The Victorian
BOOK OF CAKES

The Victorian

BOOK OF CAKES

RECIPES, TECHNIQUES AND DECORATIONS
FROM THE GOLDEN AGE OF CAKE-MAKING

BY

T. PERCY LEWIS

Chairman of Confectionery Judges, London Exhibition

AND

A. G. BROMLEY

Continental Prize Scholar, Vienna, 1897–1898

Diploma of Honour for skill and workmanship, London Exhibition 1898

WITH A

FOREWORD

BY

NICHOLAS LODGE

of the House of Sugarcraft

THE VICTORIAN BOOK OF CAKES

This edition published in 1991 by
Charles Letts and Company Limited
Diary House, Borough Road, London SE1 1DW

This edition copyright © 1991 Anness Law Ltd

This edition was produced by Anness Law Limited
4a The Old Forge
7 Caledonian Road
London N1 9DX

ISBN 1-85238-135-3

British Library Cataloguing in Publication Data
Lewis, T. Percy
    [Book of cakes]   The Victorian book of cakes.
    1.   Cakes – Recipes
    I. [Book of cakes]   I. Title
    641.8653

ISBN 1-85238-135-3

Letts is a registered trademark of Charles Letts (Scotland) Limited

Printed and bound in Hong Kong

Publisher's Note
This is a facsimile reproduction of an authentic Victorian cake recipe
book, written for professional bakers. The recipes were not intended
for home use. Therefore ingredients, quantities, methods, and
instructions are based on original professional recipes and should be
regarded as such. The notes to the modern reader contain helpful
advice on adapting recipes and the ingredients have been adjusted to
modern measurements; however, the publishers cannot guarantee
success.

CONTENTS

FOREWORD

NICHOLAS LODGE

of the House of Sugarcraft

Looking through this fascinating book takes me back to my time at college, when I searched through the antique book shops in London trying to find old books on confectionery and cake decorating. I found these books invaluable as a source of inspiration as well as for their technical information.

Many of the methods and techniques in this book have remained unchanged, despite our modern use of mixes and prepared bases. These modern preparations are not always of the same quality and flavour as their old-fashioned counterparts, but do make our lives easier, of course – and they compare favourably with some rather dubious old-fashioned practices such as, for instance, adding laundry blue to royal icing to make it white, or adding starch to icing sugar for its anti-caking properties. However, no such practices are recommended in this publication!

The Victorian Book of Cakes covers many areas of confectionery and sugarcraft, and includes the most wonderful colour plates. The details and colours of the cakes illustrated should be inspirational for any student of catering, as the ideas can be taken and adapted to make alternative designs.

The main section of the book is made up of hundreds of recipes that can be adapted for both home and commercial use. The book's appeal is very wide, and it will be of interest to anyone with a love of confectionery or sugarcraft. (I personally found the sections on shortbread and petits fours fascinating, as I often make those for gifts at Christmas time.) I hope you will browse through this volume for hours, looking for ideas and marvelling at the skills revealed.

THE BOOK OF CAKES

NOTE TO THE MODERN READER

This charming Victorian recipe collection was written by professional bakers for use by other professional bakers. Consequently, the Victorian caterers who would have first used this book wouldn't have needed any of the instructional information included in most modern cook books. This introduction contains helpful advice and information for the home cook.

Before beginning any recipe, take time to study the quantities. Some were specifically written using catering-size quantities and equipment. It is a good idea to make sure you have enough oven space and baking tins.

CAKES

Cake recipes should be followed precisely for success; substituting different types of fat or flour can cause problems, as can doubling or reducing quantities of ingredients.

GENERAL TIPS

Have all the ingredients at room temperature before starting. This helps butter and fat to cream easier, and sugar to dissolve more quickly.

Always bake cakes in the centre of a preheated oven. Bake shallow cakes higher in the oven, and deep cakes lower. Do not open the oven door during baking until the cake is set and lightly brown.

Cakes with a high proportion of rich ingredients, such as sugar or butter or fruit, should be baked at lower temperatures.

Small and thin cakes are baked at a higher temperature than large and thick cakes.

Cool cakes in their tins on the baking sheet, then transfer to a wire rack to cool completely.

Sandwich or layer cakes: these take about 25 minutes in a 350°F/175°C/Gas 4 oven for a 9 inch/23 cm tin. Bake in greased and lined shallow tins of the shape required. To test for doneness, check the edges have shrunk away from the tin and that a skewer inserted into the centre comes out clean.

Sheet and Genoese cakes: bake at 350°F/175°C/Gas 4 for about 20–30 minutes (8 inch/20 cm tin) or 30–40 minutes (10 inch/25 cm tin) until it comes away from the side of the tin and springs back when pressed. Bake in tins lined with greased paper and dusted with flour.

Fruit and wedding cakes: bake at 325°F/160°C/Gas 3 for 1–2 hours depending on the richness of the mixture – the cake should come away from the sides and a skewer inserted come out clean. Use deep round, loaf or springform tins, greased and lined with layers of greased paper.

Loaf or pound cakes: these take about 50 minutes in a 350°F/175°C/Gas 4 oven for an 8 × 4 × 3 inch/20 × 10 × 7 cm oblong loaf tin, or 45 minutes for a 9–10 inch/23–25 cm tin. Bake in greased and lined springform or loaf tins. Test for doneness by inserting a skewer into the centre (it should come out clean) about 5 minutes before the end of the recommended baking time. If the cake is browning too quickly but is still not baked, cover with foil and return to the oven.

DIAGNOSING PROBLEMS

If a cake is less successful than expected, there are a number of common causes you can check for:

Dense, solid cakes can be due to inadequate beating or whipping of the mixture (or, conversely, overmixing), or insufficient amounts of sugar and/or raising agent.

Sunken or sticky cakes can be due to undercooking, too low an oven temperature, too much raising agent or too much liquid in the mixture.

Uneven raised surfaces can be due to a too high oven temperature or overbeating the mixture.

TARTS

GENERAL TIPS

Handle pastry as little as possible. Overworking will cause the pastry to be tough when baked.

Chill the pastry after making and before rolling out. This gives the starch grains in the flour a chance to relax.

The basic proportion for shortcrust tart pastry is just over half fat to flour (5 oz/150 g to 8 oz/250 g) with 1 egg yolk and just enough cold water to bind the mixture together. This quantity fills a 10 inch/25 cm tin. Add a pinch of salt (or sugar if liked) for flavour.

Bake unfilled tart shells blind, lined with greaseproof paper and filled with baking beans, at 425°F/220°C/Gas 7 for 10 minutes, then remove the lining and beans and bake at 375°F/190°C/Gas 5 for 5–10 minutes longer or until crisp and golden.

Bake unfilled tartlet shells lined as above at 425°F/220°C/Gas 7 for about 10 minutes, then remove paper and bake for another 10 minutes, or until crisp and golden.

Filled tart and tartlet shells are baked at different temperatures, depending on their filling.

An 8 inch/20 cm tart shell requires about 2 oz/50 g of filling.

TESTING FOR DONENESS

These are simple sight and texture tests that will tell you when baked goods are ready to come out of the oven:

Cakes are done when the top springs back if lightly pressed with your fingertips and a wooden toothpick inserted in the centre comes out clean. Baked cakes will also slightly come away from the side of the tin.

Biscuits are done when they feel set and are a light golden colour all over.

Meringues are done when they are a pale fawn colour all over.

Pastries are done when they are a golden crisp colour all over.

OVEN SETTINGS

Cool oven	300°F/150°C/Gas 2	Moderately hot oven	375°F/190°C/Gas 5
Warm oven	325°F/160°C/Gas 3	Quick oven	375°F/190°C/Gas 5
Moderate oven	350°F/180°C/Gas 4	Fairly hot oven	400°F/200°C/Gas 6
Good oven	350°F/180°C/Gas 4	Hot oven	425°F/220°C/Gas 7
Sound oven	375°F/190°C/Gas 5		

UNUSUAL EQUIPMENT

The three pieces of baking equipment used in this book that may not be familiar to many modern cooks are Savoy bags, hoops and wooden frames for slab cakes.

Savoy bags are simply catering-size pastry bags, which got their name because they were used to pipe Savoy biscuits, like ladyfingers.

Hoops are large metal rings placed on baking sheets for baking cakes in. They are available from catering supply shops but a much more convenient, modern equivalent is a loose-bottomed cake tin.

If you do choose to use hoops, however, some preparation is necessary so that the cake batter does not all seep out on the baking sheet. Cut out a circle of greaseproof paper, 4 inches/10 cm wider than the diameter of the hoop. Place the hoop in the centre of the circle, and trace around the hoop with a pencil. At regular intervals snip around the circle from the edge of the paper to the tracing line. Place the paper circle inside the hoop and fold up the sides inside all round.

Fruit cakes baked in hoops, or more conventional loaf tins, sometimes need wrapping in a double thickness of brown paper before baking. This helps protect the sides of the cake from scorching during the long baking time.

Wooden frames are used for making fruit and slab cakes with rich fillings because wood does not conduct heat as much as tin and there is less chance of the side of the cake scorching. These are also available from catering supply shops, and, if you use one of these, the bottom will have to be wrapped with protective paper like the hoops.

Be sure the baking sheets you use are sturdy and thick so that they do not buckle while in the oven.

INGREDIENTS

Flours: today's flours are much more standardized than they were when this book was first written. Plain flour is suitable for most recipes. For the lighter cakes and gâteaux and pastries, however, you might like to use cake flour, which is becoming more widely available. On the label it is called 'soft' flour. This means it is made from softer grains of wheat, and produces a lighter texture.

Do not use cake flour for fruit cakes because the flour needs extra strength to stop the fruit from sinking to the bottom.

To make your own cake flour, sift together 2 tablespoons cornflour and 4 ounces/125 g plain flour less 2 tablespoons.

Boiled sugar: a sugar or candy thermometer is valuable for making anything that involves boiling sugar to an exact temperature. They are available from any good cook's shop.

If, however, you do not have a sugar thermometer, there are simple sight and touch tests. Remove the pan from the heat, and drop a little syrup into a clean cup of very cold, but not iced, water.

Thread or blow degree (235°F/113°C) – this forms a fine thread, or, if a thin wire loop is inserted in the syrup, it will come out with a thin film which can be blown.

Soft ball stage (240°F/115°C) – a small amount of the syrup sets into a ball when rubbed between the fingertips.

Hard crack stage (290°F/143°C) – a small ball of sugar syrup sets very hard and brittle, and is difficult to crack.

Unusual Ingredients

Carmine – a natural red food dye made from the crushed bodies of the female species of a certain type of insect. Today, it is known as cochineal. Substitute any edible red food colour.

Heliotrope – Victorians used this food dye to produce pale purple or reddish lavender colours. Any specialist cake-decorating shop will stock a modern equivalent.

Gum paste – professional cake decorators use this paste made from icing sugar, cornflour, powdered gum tragacanth (gum dragon) and water to make (inedible) firm cake decorations. Keep the paste well covered before moulding, as it hardens quite quickly when exposed to air. Catering supply shops often sell ready-prepared mixes (sometimes made up with water) – you can add food colours to these if required.

Powder or volatile – before baking powder and bicarbonate of soda were commercially available, bakers had to prepare their own mixtures to act as leavening agents in cakes and some biscuits.

Page 182 gives a recipe for making powder in large quantities. As a general guideline, however, mix two parts cream of tartar with one part bicarbonate of soda. Use 1½–2 teaspoons of this mixture for every 4 oz/125 g of flour.

When using one of these homemade powders be sure to have the oven preheated and all the other ingredients assembled. These chemicals react with moisture to give off carbon dioxide. This is what causes baked goods to rise and be light in texture. Unlike modern double-acting baking powders, all the reaction in these homemade versions occurs instantly.

FIRST PUBLISHER'S PREFACE

Pascal laid down the dictum that in composing a book the last thing that one learns is to know what to put first, and the authors who are responsible for the letterpress which follows have got themselves out of this difficulty by imposing upon us the duty of writing the introduction. The burden is lightened by the pleasure which is afforded in recognising and recording the willing assistance which has been given to the publishers by the authors and a small body of very willing and very able confectioners who readily agreed to supply articles from which the illustrations were taken. For a number of years it had been the ambition and the object of the publishers to produce a work upon British confectionery which would be alike creditable to the producers and valuable to the trade. They had many difficulties to contend with, and have now the satisfaction of knowing that in presenting this volume, they have been successful in producing the finest and most trustworthy book that there is upon the subject. The illustrations are unique. With the exception of the Wedding, Birthday, and other cakes belonging to that family, every illustration has been reproduced from the actual cake. In nearly every case the cake was made to our order, and special attention was directed by the makers to supply a suitable article. Most of the cakes were made by Messrs Lewis, of Malvern, in conjuction with Mr A. G. Bromley, whose special department can be easily recognised by those who have had acquaintance with the admirable work which he has done in International Exhibitions. We are also indebted to Mr W. R. Hubbard, Glasgow, for his kindness in supplying most of the Meringues illustrating Section VIII., the Charlotte Ecossaise and the Trifle in Section X.; to Mr Alexander Austin, South Street, Elgin, for supplying us with an original recipe for Shortbread and the cakes illustrated in Section VI., plates 1, 2 and 3; to Mr James Fielding, Manchester, for the excellent Simnel cake.

The beautiful Wedding cakes, all of which figured at one time or another in the prize lists of the London International Exhibitions, could not be surpassed, and we therefore decided to illustrate the section with the reproduction of photographs which were taken at the time for use in the *British Baker*. It gives us great pleasure to direct the attention of readers to the work of the different artists. In Section I., plate 1 represents a three-tier Wedding cake which gained the first prize in the Scottish Section of the Exhibition, 1902, and was the work of Mr Pass, Glasgow; plate 2 was the first prize cake in the English Section of 1901, and was the work of Mr H. G. Stiles, St Ives; plate 3 represents a two-tier Bride's cake by Mr S. P. Borella, which gained the first prize in 1902. Plate 5 in Section I. represents the first prize gained by Mr Oldham, Newark-on-Trent, in equality with another competitor in the Exhibition of 1902; and plate 6 also represents a first prize cake, the work of Mr Oldham in 1902. Plate 7 represents two cakes, the work of Mr Howell, 12 Chryssell Road, Brixton, and two which are the work of Mr Borella; and plate 8 contains illustrations of prize cakes made by Mr F. Pass, Glasgow, Mr J. D. Baillie, Glasgow, Mr Oldham, and Mr Borella.

It is needless for the publishers to say anything regarding the outstanding abilities for the joint authors. They have only to express the satisfaction with which they have collaborated in producing a work which marks an epoch in the art of confectionery, and which is destined to remain the standard work on the subject for very many years.

Maclaren & Sons Offices of "The British Baker" 37 and 38 Shoe Lane, London, E.C.

MATERIALS — THE CHOICE AND PURCHASE OF

To ensure success there is nothing of more importance in the confectionery world than a proper choice of the ingredients which are used in the manufacture of the many and various goods sold under the comprehensive name of "confectionery." It is hoped that the notes given in this chapter will be of use – not so much to the experienced buyer of raw materials, who has usually paid very dearly for his experience, but to those who have not given sufficient attention to the question before, and to those younger men who, having become artists in the manufacturing department, are now turning their attention to the strictly commerical side.

In a short chapter of this description it is unnecessary and undesirable to enter into an exhaustive chemical analysis of the different raw goods used in the bakery; and it is taken for granted that our readers will know the general appearance and characteristics of flour, sugar, eggs, etc.

Flour. – Insufficient attention is often given to the importance of using the right kind of flour for each particular class of goods.

In many bakeries, where bread and cakes are made, the foreman is most particular as to the grading of the flour for bread, but he does not consider the need of equal care in mixing and blending for the "smalls" trade. This indifference is the principal cause of the many sad-looking, dark buns, and the unevenly vesiculated cakes we see around us. Probably the most useful flour on the confectionery side is Hungarian. There are many grades of these flours on the market, and in a great many cases their marks are unreliable; but there are also numbers of good brands that can be thoroughly depended on, and one of the best of these should be chosen. It may be taken as a rule that, for confectioners' use, the two or three shillings difference between good and best flour is well spent, and is repaid with interest by the better flavour, bloom, and colour of the finished goods. For all yeast goods it is well to use a strong flour, say, Spring American Patent, with a good British milled brand, and some Hungarian, and the proportion of one part American, two parts British, one part Hungarian. The brands of British milled flour vary very much in different districts, so the best plan is to find out a really good miller whose flour suits the individual trade, and not to move about. This rule also applies to other flours and other materials. With the army of pushing salesmen calling week by week, little wonder that the trader goes astray now and then, and is tempted by volubility or low price to buy something that is nothing like as good as that which he was previously using, and with which he was beforetime well pleased. If you are thoroughly satisfied with your productions, do not change your materials.

Butter is a most important ingredient in nearly all confectionery work, and careful attention must be given to the purchase of materials in this line. Cheap or low-priced butters are to be avoided. Good quality cannot be obtained without paying for it. Different classes of butters may be used for different kinds of goods, but each must be good in its way, and should be chosen with the largest percentage of fat possible. Irish butters are usually of very good flavour, and do splendidly for pound and slab cake work, but they often require a great deal of washing and working to get rid of an excess of salt and water. This excess, of course, reduces the percentage of fat in the purchase. United States and Canadian dairies have very similar characteristics, but have not quite so good a flavour as the Irish. Reliable brands of Canadian creameries, Danish, New Zealand, and Normandy butters are on the market which combine flavour, strength, sweetness, and texture, and from these a selection may easily be made. Finnish, or Russian, of much the same character as Danish, but at a less price, may now be purchased all the year round, and this will be found suitable for nearly every purpose. For low-priced goods, for which pure butter would be too expensive, many cheaper fats are advertised. Without entering into the respective merits of these, which are often proprietary articles, it may be taken as a rule to invariably get a small sample and thoroughly test for quantity of fat, colour, flavour and smell before purchasing bulk. Pure lard is a very useful cheapening agent, and may be safely used. We may be allowed to repeat here the advice urged before. When you have the right thing "stick" to it.

Sugar is another of the raw materials which requires careful attention. Different kinds of sugar may be used for different purposes. Thus, for fermented work, good soft "pieces" may be used with advantage, as it is very sweet and easily soluble. For creaming up use a good cane castor, or failing beet, the best castor you can get. Always be careful to secure a fairly granular, free sugar which will not cake or get lumpy in the bags or barrels, and which is sufficiently coarse in the grain to make its strength felt in the creaming-up process.

Many fine granulated sugars are sold to the unwary for castor, and the wholesaler thus makes a few shillings per cwt, above its value. The granulated answers, in many cases, very well, but it is quite unnecessary to pay more than the market value for it. Granulated sugar is easily distinguished from castor sugar by careful examination with the eyes, when it will be found that the former appears to be dwarfed white crystallised sugar. For wedding cakes, in which a very dark colour is desired, some large firms use Barbadoes sugar, which is of intense sweetness, and of the same appearance, although much darker than the "pieces" already mentioned. For icing purposes use only the finest English milled icing sugar of good bright colour, and do not grudge the extra money asked for the extra fine sugars in this class.

Eggs. – If obtainable use only British fresh eggs. This advice is easy to give, but the qualification implied in the sentence is, in a large business, an absolute barrier. We seem to be very well catered for in the immense importation from countries where either the hens lay more, or the raising of poultry is in better hands than at home. The chief points in buying eggs either British or foreign are to see that they are of good size, and that the yolk is a fine rich colour. It is certain that, if really good eggs are to be bought, a fair price must be paid. It is much more economical to pay a big price for eggs that are all good, than to purchase at a low price eggs that are 30 per cent. or more bad or doubtful. The great risk of spoilt goods is not worth running. Taken generally, fresh French and Irish, by good packers, may be relied on.

Fruit. – There is no economy in buying anything at a low price (compared with the current price) in fruit. So much waste takes place in the cleaning of low-class currants, that in this alone the price is soon levelled up to that of really good stuff. In the cheapest Sultanas the colour is so bad that the great charm of this fruit – its beautiful colour is lost. For large cakes of all descriptions fine, bold, fleshy currants of a blue-black colour should be used; and for buns, scones, etc, small, shotty, but none the less fleshy, fruit should be selected. Almonds and Pistachio kernels must be chosen of a good shape and flavour, and in the case of the Pistachios, of a fine green colour; badly harvested kernels being often more yellow than green. Cherries should be of fine bright colour, preferably of a medium size. Most of the cherries used in England are imported from France, but last season we purchased some splendid fruit preserved and put up in England, and we hope, in the future, to see this industry largely develop at home.

Essences, Chemicals, and Colours. – It is not the intention of the writers to enter into the selection of essences, chemicals, or colours. In each case they should be selected pure and good. The best obtainable is a good rule to apply to goods in this class.

It seems unnecessary to summarise the foregoing notes, as in each class of goods the advice has been the same, viz. to buy good materials. The choice of these materials has been suggested, but on the individual buyer lies the onus of decision.

It is so very easy to get a collection of goods in the warehouse which are not exactly what the confectioners want; and when reflected on, it often resolves itself into the cause – over persuasion by a too pushing salesman. Buyers should always be careful not to overload themselves with any class of raw material. In these days of large refrigerators it is even unnecessary to buy and store butter as was the case a few years since; and now, with that as with everything else, unless there is some special reason for forward buying, the best plan is to buy in reasonable quantities as required.

ILLUSTRATION, PLATE I., SECTION I.

THREE-TIER WEDDING CAKE

THE illustration we give is so clear and distinct in detail that little explanation or description is necessary. It is essentially a clean, neat-looking cake of admirable colour and design, and of a decided commercial character.

In so severe a cake as this the colour must be above reproach. No dinginess or dulness must mar the brilliant white, either in icing or piping, which must exactly match. The "building up" of the borders, scrolls, and lines must be true, and, although of a comparatively simple design, any carelessness in execution would be noticeable at once.

This cake is mounted on a thick board, which is iced and piped with a sweeping scroll round the middle and a shell border above and below. The lower cake has a well-defined, built-up bottom border, which is so clearly defined in the picture that no description is necessary. Above and below this, running round the cake, are graduated straight lines with fine work waves on the inner sides.

THREE-TIER BRIDE'S-CAKE. Page 1, Section 1.

WORLD'S
FINEST FLOUR

OVER 40
AWARDS
obtained during
1902,
including 6
Champion Silver
Cups and
17 Gold Medals

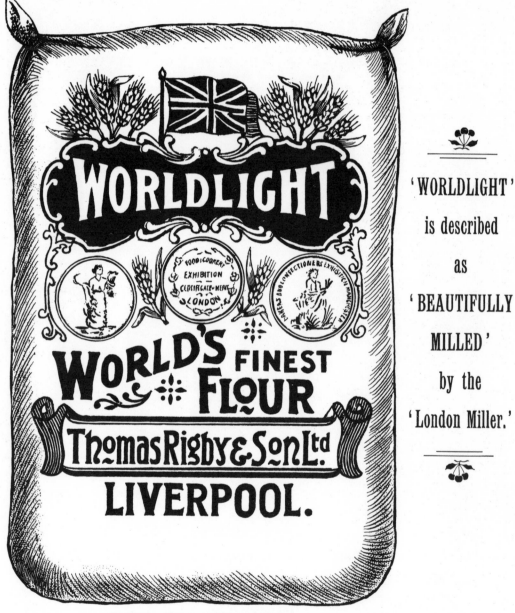

In Cotton Bags, 140 lbs., as above.

'WORLDLIGHT'
is described
as
'BEAUTIFULLY
MILLED'
by the
'London Miller.'

"WORLDLIGHT" FLOUR
USED ALONE ALWAYS INCREASES TRADE

The top border is of fine thread work, supported on circles, set up high round the cake, and finished off on the under side with built-up piping, which is shown clearly in the photo. The middle and the top cakes are executed in precisely the same style, and the whole is surmounted by a beautiful Parian vase with Cupids on each side. To those who wish to make a really high-class cake no better advice can be given than to carefully study the representation opposite, and, without copying, to follow on the lines suggested.

C

ILLUSTRATION, PLATE II., SECTION I.

THREE-TIER WEDDING CAKE

THIS is a good solid-looking wedding cake which, although it looks fairly simple of design, requires the expenditure of a considerable amount of time in its decoration.

As each tier is piped in precisely the same design, which is set out quite clearly in the illustration, it is unnecessary to give more than a superficial description of the work. The cake is mounted on a silver-edged board, which is covered with icing, and the bottom border is gradually worked out over the board. The middle design on each tier is a kind of reversed raised scroll interspersed with fine piping to fill up. The top borders are raised considerably, both on top and sides, and it is in this that so much care is required; every layer must be directly above the others. The finished cake is surmounted by a raised gum-paste basket with a handle, containing a shower bouquet.

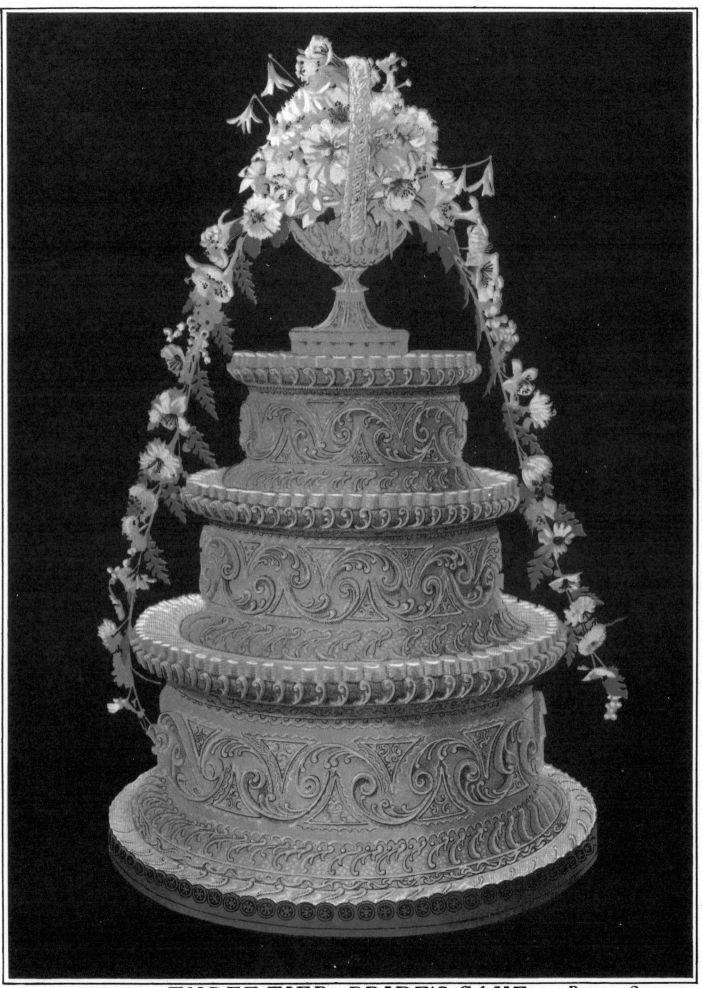

THREE-TIER BRIDE'S-CAKE. Page 2, Section 1.

ILLUSTRATION, PLATE III., SECTION I.

TWO-TIER WEDDING CAKE

THIS cake, although not absolutely inimitable, is practically so to the everyday workman. Such work, although attempted by many, has only been successfully carried out by the artist from whose creation the photograph is taken. Both top and bottom tiers are slightly higher than the conventional idea, and this allows, in this case, of open spaces, which afford the necessary relief to the fine work and decoration of the borders. Most of the detail in this cake lies in the borders, which are artistically crowded, principally with delicate lace and embroidery work done off the cake. It is unnecessary to give a complete description of the work on this cake, as every detail is reproduced in the illustration; but it must be impressed on the reader that no portion of the decoration is executed in moulded gum paste, the work being piping from start to finish.

The board on which it stands is a little larger than the cake, and is attached by carrying out the border of the cake, by means of a curve, to the extreme edge of the board. This border is composed of thread and embroidery work standing out at different angles from the cake; surmounted by festoons piped on, and is finished off at the bottom by a pretty scroll. There is no design round the middle of the cake, the plain surface giving an amount of relief, necessary to show up the excellence of the work in the borders. The top border of the bottom cake is built out with a series of six sets of circular piping, held together, and in position, by lace work; between each of these sets falls a spray of lightly piped ivy leaves. Immediately below, and forming part of the top border, runs a graceful design in festoons and lace work, descending to a point on the side of the cake between each ivy spray. The top cake is very similar in character, though different in design. The sides are piped with small monograms, and the top border is incurved with circular work in thread and lace, and is surmounted with pointed, curved leaves standing up like a crown.

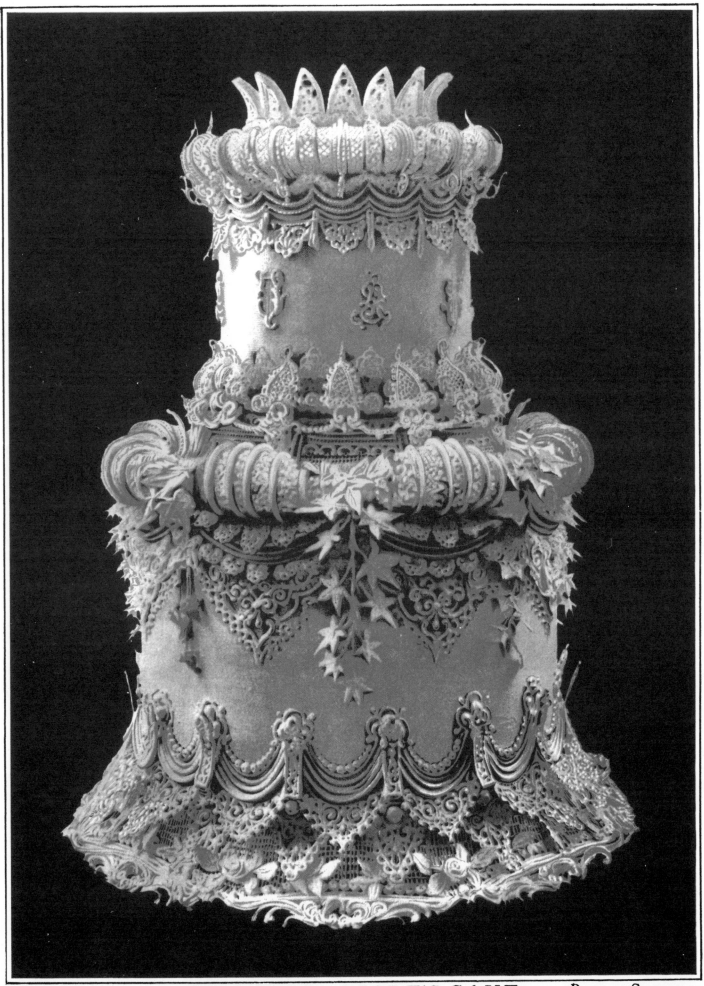

TWO-TIER BRIDE'S-CAKE. Page 3, Section I.

ILLUSTRATION, PLATE IV., SECTION I.

TWO-TIER WEDDING CAKE

THIS cake is given as an example of the use of pillars in building up the tiers, and one way of using gum-paste ornaments
and silver paper leaves. Generally we do not advise the wholesale
use of these things in cake decoration. There are many reasons, in a
cake of this description, why "artificial" ornamentation should not
be used. In the first place, it is very seldom that the colour of the
icing sugar exactly matches that of the gum paste bought from a
sundries-man; still less often does the character of the piping work
correspond in the slightest detail with the paste work. To describe
the cake in the illustration: The lower tier is a mass of built-up coarse
thread work in spindle shapes, divided through the middle by rows
of stars, which are run round the cake. Every available spot, where
the thread work is not, is carefully filled with a small piped rose and
some fern-like variety of silver leaf. The upper border, which is composed of piped loops, is partially covered with favours, leaves, and
four gum-paste slippers containing white flowers. The upper tier,

which is raised from the lower by four gum-paste pillars, is piped in a much too heavy manner, and without any regard for the appearance of the bottom portion. The work on this tier consists simply of top and bottom borders. The bottom border, which reaches nearly one third up the side of the cake, is piped very coarsely in an irregular scroll design of uncertain origin. The top border, which in its turn is made to nearly meet the lower border, is of thread-work supported below with festoons and divided into sections with silver leaves and artificial flowers. A large gum-paste vase with bouquet surmounts the whole.

TWO-TIER BRIDE'S-CAKE.

PAGE 4, SECTION 1.

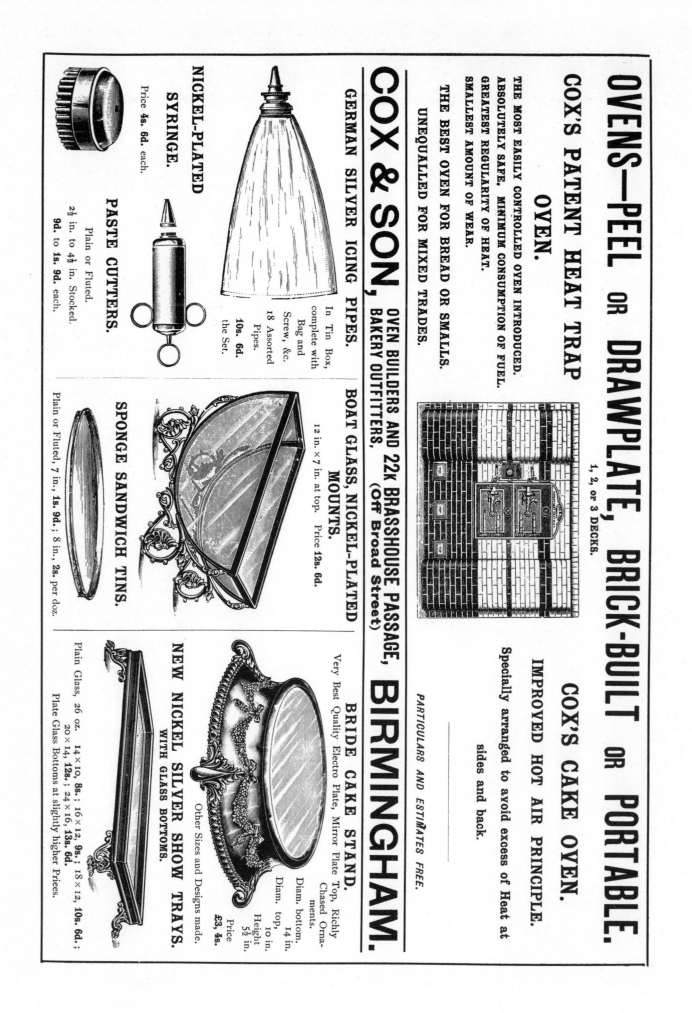

ILLUSTRATION, PLATE V., SECTION I.

GOLDEN WEDDING CAKE

THE picture given is an excellent example of a cake which in every line and decoration is suggestive of the occasion for which it is intended. The treatment of the subject shows what can be done when the workman never for a moment loses sight of the ultimate purpose of his work and builds up idea upon idea until it becomes a triumphant whole.

Description :—The bottom and top tier have been carefully chosen with regard to proportion, and the icing is a clear, brilliant white. The bottom border, composed of a wreath of oak leaves and acorns, intertwined with a graceful ribbon, is composed of gum-paste. On the outside fold of the ribbon is piped in Old English the words " Health," " Wealth," " Happiness," etc., the writing being topped with gold. Round the middle of the bottom cake runs a stucco band, divided into four by shields, on two of which monograms are piped, and on the others, " 50 years." On the stucco band, in the four divisions between the shields, appears " Heaven, bless our Golden

Wedding," also in Old English and topped with gold. Some light lacework, done with a fine pipe above the band, gives this cake a furnished appearance. The top border is composed of gum-paste ivy leaves set out from the cake, but close together and irregular, with a row of piped leaves pointing down on the side of cake. On the top cake we have a nice piece of work in the centre band, which is divided into quarters, in the same way as the lower cake, by four moulded lions' heads, in the mouth of each of which is hung a gold ring. Between the lions there is some very good scroll piping, and above and below the centre band is the same style of lace-piping as appears on the bottom cake. The top border is composed of wheat in the full ear in gum-paste, attached as in the other tier, with the exception that the ends of the ears point in the opposite direction.

The whole is surmounted by a Parian vase, with a bouquet of yellow roses, and streamers falling over the sides of cake.

To ensure success in the conception and execution of such a cake requires besides a considerable amount of technical knowledge, care, thought and the exercise of a well-trained imagination. Every detail must be attended to, and the icing, gum-paste and piping must be exactly of the same colour.

GOLDEN WEDDING CAKE. Page 5, Section 1.

ILLUSTRATION, PLATE VI., SECTION I.

SILVER WEDDING CAKE

THIS is a bold-looking cake, and will give a very good general idea of a well-conceived silver wedding cake. The cake, which stands on a wooden base with silver edging, is iced in white, and gum-paste enters very largely into the scheme of decoration. (Care should be taken to ensure that the colour of icing and gum-paste is precisely the same.) The bottom border is made of moulded gum-paste, as also are the four circular panels or medallions which are on the sides of the cake. These medallions have raised moulded borders with silver lace paper edging, and stucco centres; on this stucco work is piped in Old English "Silver Wedding" on two, and "25 Years" on the other two. Resting on the bottom border, between the medallions, are four semi-circular stages, each carrying a small silver goblet which holds white flowers. The bottom half of the cake is finished by heavy built-up piping around and beneath the large medallions and by flowers and foliage artistically strewed about.

D

The upper part of the cake is finished in much the same way as the lower. Immediately above the circular panels on the sides, there are ornate scroll designs worked up to form a part of the border. The remainder of the border is composed of gum-paste flower-holders in which are placed flowers and foliage. The top is finished with a small drum surmounted by a silver-plated centre representing a cupid, seated on a raised cornucopia, reaching out for a butterfly.

SILVER WEDDING CAKE.

ILLUSTRATION, PLATE VII., SECTION I.

ONE-TIER WEDDING CAKES

THE cakes illustrated on this sheet were originally piped and shown as Birthday, Christmas, etc., but as, in decoration, they are generally suitable for Wedding Cakes, they are now shown as such.

The two top cakes contain some very fine work, and are altogether more pretentious than the bottom ones. From a careful study of the work in these four cakes, many ideas may be picked up, which will prove useful in decorating cakes in this very commercial line. One-tier cakes may of course be made in any size, and of late it has become more usual for all cakes, except the most expensive, to be made in this form. Those in the illustration were all of small size, but the general schemes shown may be enlarged and elaborated. The descriptions given below may not be exactly accurate as to the original cakes, but are given as a guide to the piping of one-tier cakes.

No. 1 (left hand top) is a splendidly piped cake—some of

the work is done off the cake and afterwards fastened on, and this adds to the lightness and beauty of the design or designs. The bottom border, which is outcurved to the edge of the board, is composed of fine thread-work divided into sections by a lyre-like scroll design, which being carried under the thread-work makes a finish to the border. Underneath the scroll is piped a series of graduated dots, which are effective.

The design for the top border is the principal scheme of the cake. Between the top and the bottom border is just sufficient open space to give relief to the elaborate upper half of the cake.

The top border is practically divided into sections by square points or triangles, with lines finely graduated, and edges scroll piped. From the top of the cake and falling over each triangle is placed an outcurved piped leaf, and between these the edge of the border is completed by a piped rose and scroll work. To fill up the space between the points of triangles a mixture of thread-work, plain festoons, and fine border piping is used with excellent effect.

No. 2 (right hand top). This cake is very similar in general idea to No. 1, and the description of the one bottom border will do for both cakes. The graduated irregular lines above the bottom border and the festoons under the upper border are very effective, as

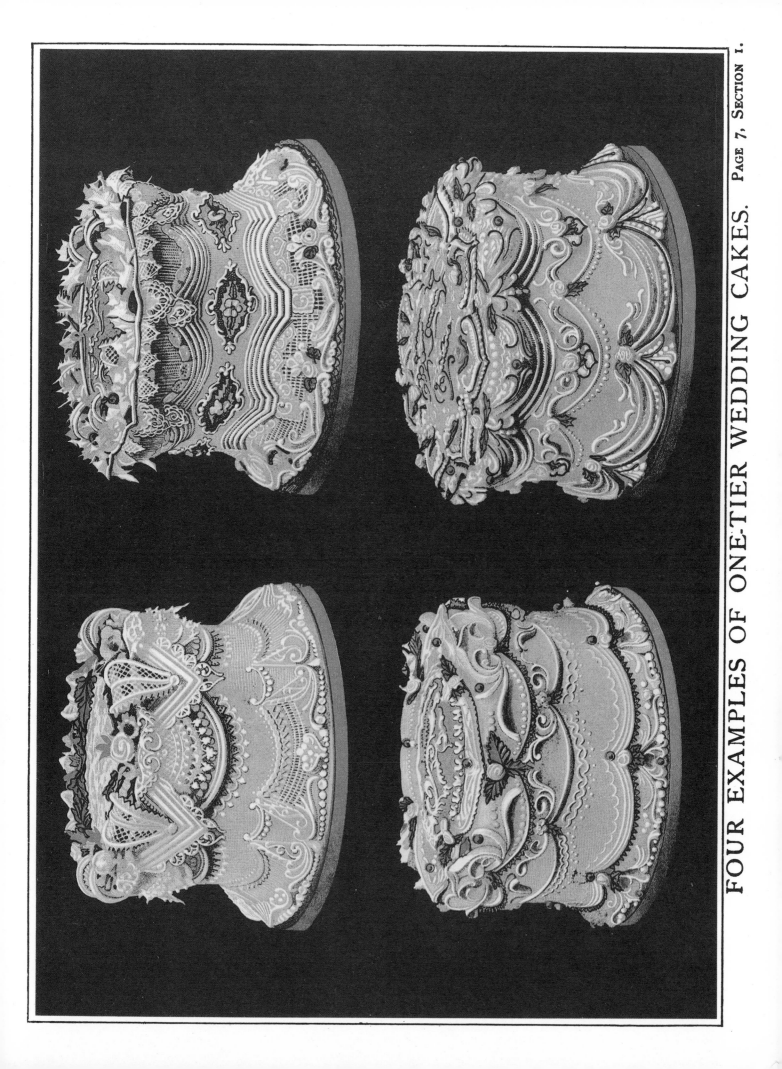

FOUR EXAMPLES OF ONE-TIER WEDDING CAKES. PAGE 7, SECTION I.

ERNEST SCHÜLBE'S

Confectioners' School of Art.

62

Wilmslow Road

WITHINGTON,

MANCHESTER.

62

Wilmslow Road

WITHINGTON,

MANCHESTER.

FIRST PRIZE:

Gold Medal again Awarded, Manchester Exhibition 1897.

BEATING THE LONDON CHAMPION CUP WINNER.

LESSONS GIVEN

WITH GREAT SUCCESS

In Piping, Modelling in Gum Paste and Marzipan, Fancy Pastries, Meringues, Sugar Spinning, or anything connected with artistic Confectionery.

✿

BEST SYSTEM OF TEACHING.

Great Success of Pupils at all Exhibitions.

✿

Bride Cake Dummies

A SPECIALITY.

✿

BOOK OF DESIGNS:

"CAKE DECORATION,"

5/-, Post Free 5/4.

FINEST AND STRONGEST

BRASS PIPING TUBES.

5/-, 6/-, and 7/- per Set, sent post free.

✿

Revolving Stands

7s. EACH.

The Best Invention, the Most Perfect, the Strongest and Cheapest in the Market.

Canvas Savoy Bags.

Rubber Bags with Dopple Screw.

Meringue Tubes, all kinds and Shapes.

✿

VEGETABLE FLOWER CUTTERS.

Remarkably Easy to Use, 2/6 per Set.

✿

Parian and Gum=Paste Ornaments

ALWAYS IN STOCK.

Box of Half-Dozen Modelling Tools (Wood), 4s. 6d.

Box of One Dozen Ivory Modelling Tools, 10s. 6d.

New Hollow Net Tins for Piping, Three Shapes, Seven Sizes, 6d. each, 5s. per Dozen.

also are the small panels round the centre of the cake. The top border was originally composed of piped white holly-leaves, and although this may not be quite suitable for a wedding cake, those who like the idea may substitute leaves that would satisfy their preconceived ideas of wedding-cake decoration. The immediate edge is made up of outcurved piped leaves just overhanging the side of the cake.

No. 3 is a much more simple cake to execute by the everyday workman. The illustration is an excellent one, and every line being shown it makes description unnecessary. Festoons in graduated lines, with simple scrolls built up, form the chief part of the design, and a discreet use of small silver leaves will commend itself to many people who like to see silver leaves on a white cake.

No. 4 is essentially a festoon cake. Most of the available space is filled up with small independent scroll designs, and a liberal use of sugar roses and silver leaves completes the scheme.

ILLUSTRATION, PLATE VIII., SECTION I.

CHRISTMAS, BIRTHDAY AND CHRISTENING CAKES

THE four cakes illustrated on this sheet will give a good idea of first-class work under the above heading. It is necessary to impress on the reader the fact that in all this kind of work, great care should be taken in the selection of the materials to be used in decoration. In all cakes in which colour forms part of the scheme of adornment, the exercise of considerable taste is essential to ensure elegant work. The general effect of many cakes, which are in other ways excellent, is entirely spoilt by the use of either too much colour, too many mixed colours, or bad colour. The sheet of illustration contains one Christmas Cake (No. 4); two Birthday Cakes (Nos. 1 and 2); and one Christening Cake (No. 3).

BIRTHDAY CAKE, No. 1

This cake was originally iced in pale pink, and was placed on

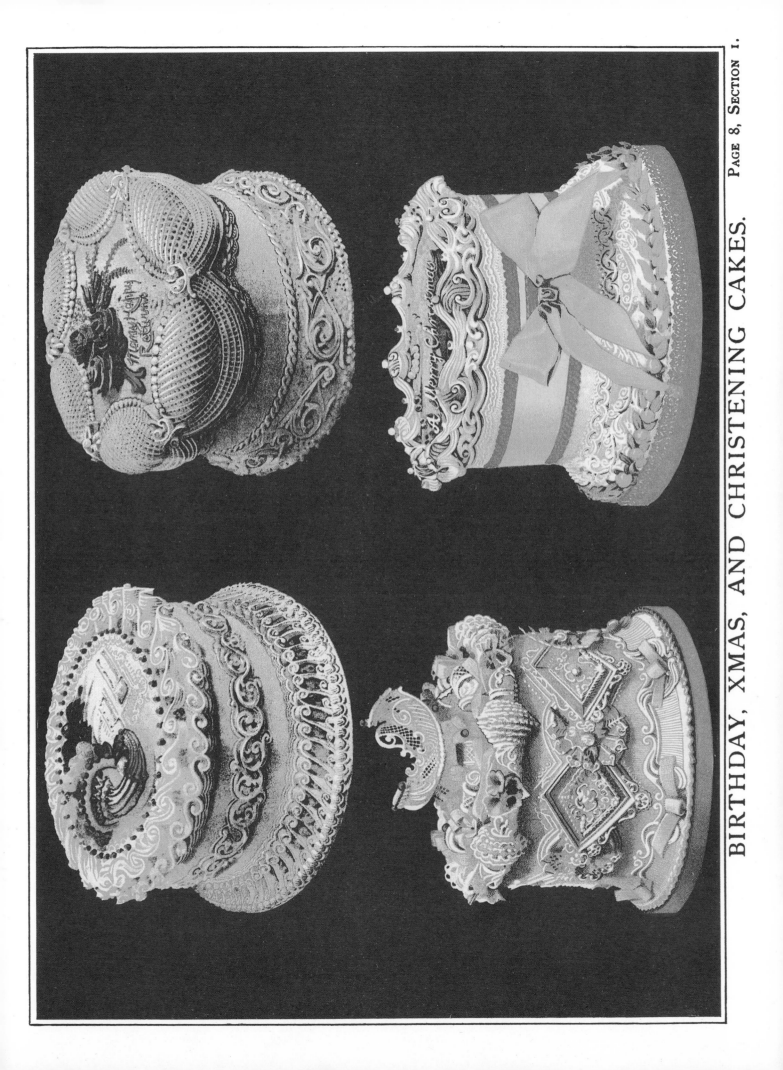

BIRTHDAY, XMAS, AND CHRISTENING CAKES.

a board which was covered with icing. The bottom border was worked down on to the edge of the board forming a gentle curve. The sides are piped round the centre with a rather close scroll design, worked up. The plain icing showing above and below gives the necessary relief to the heavy piping. The top border, which is fairly heavy, is a simple scroll, built up round the outer edge, and repeated on top on the inner edge. On the top of the cake inside this are placed in a circle small pieces of crystallised violets, and the centre is completed by placing on a decorated cornucopia containing a spray of flowers, and by writing a suitable inscription on a ribbon ground. The whole of the piping is in white.

BIRTHDAY CAKE, No. 2

This cake is iced entirely in white, with pink piping. The bottom border is piped on a sloping stucco base, which is graduated out on to the board. The piping consists of an excellent scroll, free and graceful. Above this is a clear space which relieves the heavy work on the upper part. The top border is composed of six sections of raised overstrung work very evenly done, and the centre of the top contains a spray of yellow roses and leaves, with " many happy returns " piped underneath. The roses are piped, and practically the whole of the other decoration on the cake is done with different sized plain tubes.

CHRISTENING CAKE, No. 3

This cake is much more elaborate than either of the preceding, from a workman's point of view. To produce anything like this requires much time, skill and artistic ability. The cake stands on a silver-edged board, and is iced and piped in white, the only touch of colour being the small bows of cream-coloured ribbon which form part of the decoration. Much of the work is done off the cake, particularly in the top border and the cradle, which is an excellent example of artistic thread-piping. The bottom border is divided into sections of fine work surrounded by scroll which graduates outward on to the board. The middle of the cake is a very elaborate design in diamonds and part circles. The top border is also divided into sections, and by open ribbon work is built up to the cradle which is raised on rockers.

CHRISTMAS CAKE, No. 4

This is a most effective cake, both in colour and design. The original from which the illustration was taken was much more striking in its bold colouring. The sides were iced in white, with a wide gold-edged band, round which was a red or crimson ribbon tied in a large bow. The large bottom border graduated out to the board, was piped in scroll, and the outer edge finished with cherries and angelica, which made an effective band right round the cake. The top was iced in sage-green, with the writing in rustic letters done in coffee colour. There were also sprays of holly and mistletoe and fruit to complete the top decoration. The top border was bold, built-up scroll, with fine wavy piping falling in festoons down the side of cake.

WEDDING CAKES

5 lbs. Butter

4½ lbs. Sugar (Barbadoes advised)

6¼ lbs. Eggs

5 lbs. Flour

4 lbs. Chopped Citron Peel

4 lbs. Orange Peel

5 lbs. Sultanas

15 lbs. Currants

4 Grated Lemons

1 Grated Nutmeg

½ oz. Mixed Spice

¼ oz. Mace

2 ozs. Cut Almonds

½ pint Brandy

½ pint Rum.

GET all the ingredients ready before starting the mixing. Cream up the butter and sugar well, and add the eggs, a few at a time, thoroughly beating between each lot. Stir in the fruit and flour until it is all well mixed. It is advisable to mix in the fruit before the flour, thus preventing any floury fruit showing in the cake when cut. The rum should be added to the mixing, but the brandy may, if thought proper, be added by pouring on the cakes immediately on their being taken from the oven. If the cake is required to be very dark in colour, a small quantity of " black jack," or burnt sugar, may be added and beaten well into the mixing. As these cakes require a good deal of baking, the hoops, after being prepared with bands in the usual way, should be placed on several thicknesses of brown paper or on a layer of bran on a baking-sheet. This will effectively prevent the bottom of the cakes scorching. The cakes should be baked in a moderately cool oven, as the taste of burnt fruit is particularly objectionable in bride cakes. In businesses of any size where this class of cake is in fair demand, a supply should be kept ready made, as by keeping they become mellow and, to a certain extent, improve in quality. If the fruit is properly prepared and dried there is little limit to the keeping quality of a well-made wedding cake.

WEDDING CAKE, No. 2

(CHEAPER)

3 lbs. Butter

3 lbs. Sugar

3 Eggs

5 lbs. Flour

10 lbs. Currants

2 lbs. Sultanas

3 lbs. Peel (Lemon and Orange mixed)

2 ozs. Spice

Rum.

THIS cake is somewhat cheaper than No. 1, having more flour in its composition. It consequently requires a larger quantity of darkening to make its appearance right, but otherwise the remarks and directions in No. 1 apply in this case.

CHRISTMAS CAKES

UNLIKE bride cakes, there is no hard-and-fast rule as to the particular class of mixing to be used for Christmas cakes. The general idea at this time of year is to make something of the rich fruity order, but when, as is the case with a large percentage of Christmas cake, it is to be a eaten by children, the business of the confectioner is to introduce such cakes as may be freely eaten by clients of all ages. Recipes are given here for three different qualities of dark fruit cake, and for a sultana cake, which is in great request for nurseries. Christmas cakes may also be made of plain Madeira, cherry, or practically any mixing, in these cases relying on the finish and decorations to give the cake distinctive " Christmassy " character.

1. CHRISTMAS CAKE

3 lbs. Butter

3 lbs. Sugar

3 lbs. 10 ozs. Eggs

$3\frac{1}{2}$ lbs. Flour

$\frac{3}{4}$ lb. Patent Flour

10 lbs. Currants.

$1\frac{1}{2}$ lbs. Almonds

5 lbs. Peel

A little Spice.

Cream up the butter and sugar, and beat in the eggs in the usual way. Stir in the flour, fruit, etc., and thoroughly mix. Fill into papered cake hoops, which are placed on well-covered baking-sheets. Bake in a moderate oven.

2. CHRISTMAS CAKE

This is a much cheaper line.

$1\frac{1}{2}$ lbs. Mixture

$1\frac{1}{2}$ lbs. Sugar

1 lb. Eggs

3 lbs. Flour

1 oz. Powder (bare weight)

1 pint Milk

2 lbs. Currants

$\frac{1}{2}$ lb. Sultanas

$\frac{1}{2}$ lb. Peel.

Cream up the butter and sugar, and beat in the eggs. Mix thoroughly in the other ingredients, and give a good work up. Fill into hoops, and bake as directed for No. 1, but in a warmer oven.

3. CHRISTMAS CAKE

This recipe is included for the benefit of those who have to compete with factory-made Christmas cakes, which are sold in large numbers iced and piped at one shilling each. It may not be a class of trade which many confectioners would care to cultivate, but the exigencies of modern business may and often do compel people to act in opposition to their desires.

> 3 lbs. Sugar
>
> 2 lbs. Mixture
>
> 1½ lbs. Eggs
>
> 6 lbs. Flour
>
> 3 ozs. Powder
>
> 3 lbs. Currants
>
> 1½ lbs. Sultanas
>
> 1 lb. Peel
>
> Spice
>
> Colour
>
> Milk.

Cream up butter and sugar, and beat in the eggs. Mix in the other ingredients, and add sufficient milk to make it of a fairly soft consistency. Fill into suitably sized hoops, or tins (papered), and bake in a moderate oven. This cake should, when baked, be practically flat on top, so that no difficulty should be experienced in coating the top with icing.

4. CHRISTMAS CAKE (SULTANA)

3 lbs. Butter

3 lbs. Sugar

1 quart Eggs

3½ lbs. Flour

3 lbs. Sultanas.

Cream up butter and sugar; add the eggs in the usual way. Mix in the flour and fruit, and fill into suitably-sized hoops. Bake in a moderate oven.

BIRTHDAY AND CHRISTENING CAKES

CAKES made under these names have no distinctive feature —beyond their decoration—from any other cake. Almost any mixing will do for either. As most birthday cakes are eaten by children, it is well when taking a birthday cake order to enquire as to the ages of those for whom it is intended, and then to select a suitable class of cake. Sponge cakes are often used for this purpose for quite young children, and between this and the rich fruit of the wedding cake order there are many stages. Christening cakes, which are usually for the use of older people, are commonly made of a good rich fruit mixing, such as the following :—

> 1 lb. Butter
>
> 1 lb. Sugar
>
> 1 lb. 2 ozs. Flour
>
> 1½ lbs. Eggs
>
> 1 lb. Sultanas
>
> 1 lb. Peel
>
> 2 lbs. Currants
>
> ½ lb. Almonds (cut up)
>
> Little Rum.

Cream up the butter and sugar, and beat in the eggs. Mix in the flour, fruit, and rum, and fill into suitably-sized papered hoops. Bake in a moderately cool oven.

This recipe is, of course, for the best class of Christening cake, and, if cheaper is needed, may be easily altered to suit requirements.

Icing and Decoration of Wedding, Christmas, Birthday, and Christening Cakes

All the above cakes, if of sufficient price, should be covered with a layer of almond paste. In the cases of Wedding and Christening

F

cakes this is essential, but in Birthday and Christmas cakes much latitude is allowed, and it depends entirely upon the price or quality of the cake.

Almond Paste can be made in various ways and of many qualities. Either whole eggs, yolks of eggs, whites of eggs, or gelatine, may be used for moistening up; and the finished paste in each of these methods presents a distinctive appearance in colour.

Almond Icing may also be made without the use of any part of the egg or gums, by using boiled sugar, or, again, by working a quantity of sugar into some prepared marzipan paste.

1. *Almond Paste*

2 lbs. Sugar

2 lbs. Almonds (ground)

Sufficient yolk of egg to make a firm paste.

2. *Almond Paste*

2 lbs. Sugar

$1\frac{1}{2}$ lbs. Ground Almonds

Sufficient whites of egg to make a firm paste.

3. *Almond Paste*

2 lbs. Sugar

1 lb. Ground Almonds

Sufficient egg to make a firm paste.

In making up any of the above, it is only necessary to work the ingredients well on the board until the paste is properly mixed. For ordinary work castor sugar alone will do well, and if slightly warmed before use, the paste will set fairly hard. If a finer, smoother paste is required, icing sugar may be used, or, better still, a mixture of castor and icing sugars, which gives the paste just sufficient grain to keep it from doughiness. Good ground almonds must be used; the cheap, or rather low priced, goods in this line are not worth attention. For flavouring almond paste, a small quantity of some good liqueur should be used—unless it is good, it is better omitted, for the flavour of good almonds is far preferable to that of bad spirit. A favourite flavour for almond paste for Wedding cakes is orange flower water, and this is possibly most in keeping with established ideas. The moistening agents in each of the foregoing recipes may be interchanged.

For cheaper cakes the following recipe and method may be

used, and although it requires more care at the outset, it is easily worked into, and very quickly applied to the cakes. Cakes to be covered with this paste should be left overnight in the hoops in which they are baked.

>6 lbs. of Sugar (Cane Cubes)
>
>1 pint Water
>
>3 lbs. Almonds
>
>A pinch of Cream of Tartar.

Put the sugar, water, and cream of tartar in a clean copper stew-pan and boil to soft ball. Rub the boiled sugar on the side of pan with a spatula for a few minutes to slightly grain. Stir in the ground almonds with a little orange flower water, and at once pour over the cakes to the required thickness. Care must be taken not to boil too much, or to spend too much time in stirring afterwards, or the mixture may become too thick. If this method is preferred for better-class cakes, the above recipe may be used with the addition of 10 or 12 yolks of eggs beaten in with the almonds. The added yolks enrich the paste and make it easily workable.

With the exception of the boiled sugar recipe, for which instructions have been given, the other pastes may be put on the cakes by rolling out with a pin and carefully levelling the top and making edges quite even. The cake is now ready for receiving its first coat of sugar icing, although, when convenient, it is well to allow the almond paste to dry on the cake for some hours before covering.

Whites Icing, or Royal Icing

Icing Sugar

Whites of Eggs

Blue

Acetic Acid

Break the necessary number of whites into a clean bowl and add just sufficient icing sugar to make a very slack paste. (It is very important that too much sugar should not be put in the first, or, indeed, at any stage, but owing to the varying sizes and strengths of whites of eggs, it is misleading to state any definite number of eggs to the pound of sugar.)

Spot in a little glacial acetic acid and a few drops of liquid blue to bring the colour up bright. Beat up well with a strong wooden spatula. The most common mistake in making icing is that of being sparing of work in the beating; and to get good results it must be a rule that the icing be beaten up very light. The extra time required for this operation is well expended. When about half beaten, sprinkle in just enough sugar to make of the proper consistency when finished, and continue beating. When the icing is ready for use it should be light and smooth, and should stand stiffly in whatever position it is put.

ICING THE TOP OF CAKE.

There are many substitutes for whites of eggs, but strong and fairly fresh whites are the most convenient. By "fairly fresh" is meant whites that have been broken out perhaps for a day or two, and have consequently lost a percentage of moisture, and thus have increased the proportion of albumen.

If icing powders are used, directions will most probably accompany each packet. Generally the method is to use 2 to 4

ICING THE SIDE OF CAKE.

ozs. (according to strength) of powder to 1 pint of hot water. Dissolve the powder in the water, and stir occasionally until it is quite cold. The preparation is then ready for use in the same manner as whites of eggs.

When the icing is ready, place the cake on a silvered board and give it one good rough coating of icing. Set aside to dry thoroughly; and, when dry, proceed to give the cake its final coat. A revolving stand or turn-table is necessary to get large cakes properly iced. Two illustrations are given of a cake, on a revolving stand, being iced; the position of the palette knife being important in getting the sides upright and smooth. Perfection in icing cakes can only be attained by practice; and no amount of written instructions will do more than make suggestions to the man who will practise. The above method of icing with Royal Icing is always used in Wedding cakes, usually on Christening cakes, and sometimes on Birthday and Christmas cakes. The only drawback in the use of Royal Icing for cakes, is that it sets very hard, and is not particularly nice to eat. To do away with this difficulty, especially in such popular cakes as Birthday and Christmas, it is becoming more and more the custom to coat cakes of this kind with fondant.

Fondant for Cakes—Recipe and Method

The utensils required for fondant making are a good sized copper stew-pan with lid, a clean smooth slab, four iron bars of about 1 inch square, a strong wooden spatula, and a scraper. If not expert with boiling sugar, the reader is advised to procure a sugar-boiler's thermometer, which is marked with the degrees Fahrenheit, together with special terms used in sugar boiling. The sugar used should be a good cane sugar, either cubes or crushed being most convenient.

> 14 lbs. Sugar
>
> 3 pints Water
>
> 1 lb. Glucose (or $\frac{1}{4}$ oz. Cream of Tartar).

Place the ingredients in a copper stew-pan on the fire to boil. Boil to the soft ball degree, which is determined by dipping the fingers first into cold water, then quickly into the boiling sugar, and again into the water. The sugar on the hand may then be rubbed between the fingers, when, if at the right degree, it will be found to readily form itself into a soft smooth ball, which can easily be pressed into shape. The sugar is usually boiled without a lid on the pan, but it is convenient to just put the lid on for a minute before it is ready, when the steam will run down the sides of the pan, and clear away any crystallisation which may have appeared on the edges of the boiling sugar. Allow the sugar, when ready, to stand aside whilst the slab is being prepared. This is done by sprinkling the face of the slab with water, and by placing the iron bars in position to form a square or oblong enclosure, into which the sugar is poured. Pour the sugar in and sprinkle lightly with water, allowing it some time (about forty minutes) to partly cool; the time allowed depends on the temperature of the surrounding.   Then with the spatula, work the sugar backwards and forwards, and up and down, on the slab, until it becomes first of a soft, and then of a stiff, creamy consistency.   Store away in jars for use as required.   Any colours or flavours may be added at the time of using the fondant.

To cover with fondant, take sufficient good coloured fondant in a stew-pan, and warm up until it is just of such consistency that it may be poured over the cake.   The icing should not be so hot that it loses its natural gloss, but it should be warm enough to set readily.   If the fondant should be too stiff, and would therefore require too much heat to get it to the right consistency, the stiffness may be corrected by adding a little simple syrup.

The next matter is the actual decoration of the cake.   To commence with Wedding cakes, it is not the intention of the writers to set out any particular style of piping or other embellishment for cakes.   It is a matter for regret that styles are becoming too much "specialised," and that the majority of cakes piped by the rising talent in the trade are easily recognisable to the observant as being of so-and-so's style, and are probably either good or bad copies of another man's work.   This fact may easily be verified by an inspection of the decorative classes at the large trade exhibitions, when it will be found that cakes illustrated and described in trade books and papers are reproduced as like as possible to the original. For example, some years ago a firm in the south of England exhibited a fine Birthday cake, with a certain name nicely written on it; naturally this cake was photographed and reproduced in the trade press (thus coming into the hands of everybody), with the result that practically each year since the same name and somewhat of the same cake has reappeared, piped by first one man and then another.

It is admittedly difficult in these days to be original, but cake decoration is still very much in its infancy, and certainly there is plenty of scope for ingenuity and originality among artistic pipers.

The photographs of Wedding cakes shown earlier are purposely selected from different styles, to give the learner an idea of various kinds of work. They should certainly not be blindly copied in any case, but if each illustration is carefully studied, it will broaden the decorative idea much more than if a particular style or styles were extensively illustrated and minutely described.

The first requisites for a good piper and decorator are a good eye for colour, a natural as well as a cultivated artistic taste, and a fair knowledge of free-hand and geometrical drawing. The latter is not absolutely essential, as many really good pipers are without this branch of education; but a good grounding of School of Art work is very useful, particularly if one aims at anything like original work. It is advisable when commencing a Wedding cake to set out the design before starting work. This may be drawn on paper, by sketching in the outline of a cake of the requisite number of tiers, and then drawing on the design. By so doing one common mistake is avoided, viz. that of adding bits of piping which are not of the same style, and consequently often spoiling an otherwise tasteful work. Many men take the pipes in their hands to start work on a cake without in the least knowing beforehand what design they are going to execute. With the preliminary knowledge stated above, there is no reason why every aspiring learner should not become a fine artist, provided he is prepared to do the necessary drudgery and groundwork before attempting the more pretentious and elaborate Wedding cakes. The infallible rule to get on as a piper and decorator is to practise with brains, and to practise assiduously. Sugar for piping is prepared precisely in the same way as sugar for icing, but it is very essential that the icing should be perfectly smooth, stiff, and light. The operation necessary to ensure this result has already been described.

Gum paste is, or rather has been, considerably used in several ways in the decoration of cakes, and of late there appears to have been an effort made in some quarters to reintroduce its use on a large scale. This is somewhat a matter for regret, as most of this work is done by the mechanical means of moulding, which, unless the workman should happen to be a skilled modeller, would mean the use of other men's designs and workmanship.

If this argument, which is purely sentimental, is not sufficient, it is only necessary to examine the masterpieces in each method to determine the fact that, for artistic beauty, gum-paste work does not compare at all favourably with pure piping work. For the benefit of those who are anxious to experiment with gum-paste, a recipe is included for its manufacture—

Gum Dragon

Icing Sugar

Starch.

Take the requisite quantity, say, a few ounces, of fine picked white gum dragon, and, after carefully seeing that no impurities are in it, put to soak in a basin of water for eighteen hours. When examined then, it will be found to be quite soft and smooth. Squeeze all the water away by straining through muslin, and proceed to rub in on a scrupulously clean slab, icing sugar and fine starch in the proportion of three sugar to one of starch. When it is found that no more sugar, etc., can be rubbed in, and the paste is clear and smooth, it is ready for use, and may be formed into whatever is required. This paste is very useful for shields, panels, etc., which may be cut out in any shape required from a sheet of gum paste rolled out of the necessary thickness. All gum-paste work must be allowed to dry before being used in the decoration of a cake.

For Christening cakes custom has ordained that only white piping and decoration shall be used, so that with the exception of the top, the work is very much like that used for Wedding cakes. For the top it is sometimes customary to neatly pipe in white the name or initials of the child; others prefer a gum-paste cradle (obtained at any sundries shop) simply placed on the middle of the cake. The former idea is to be commended, as it lends variety and individuality to the cake.

For Christmas and Birthday cakes much more latitude is allowed both in style and colour of decoration. A study must be made of colours, so that no two or more colours may be used which do not blend. Lovely effects may be obtained by the careful mixing and blending of colours, and in this point many, otherwise good workmen, fail.

Always remember to use the best colours obtainable. Crystallised fruit of all kinds may be used in Christmas and Birthday cakes, and for fondant covered cakes nothing is nicer than a judicious arrangement of bright fruit cut up into suitable sizes and shapes. In this way borders and wreaths may be made and centres finished. Crystallised violets and lilac may also be used with good effect in border work.

At various times cakes have been invented for other seasons and occasions, such as the Golden Wedding Cake (Sec. I., plate 5), the Silver Wedding Cake (Sec. I., plate 6), Bridesmaid Cake and Betrothal Cake; but with the exception of the first two, which are only a partial success, they do not seem to have taken the public fancy at all. It would certainly be to the advantage of the confectioner if the latter two were taken up by the public—as there are many bridesmaids and more betrothals—but where there is Bridesmaid there is also Wedding cake, and it is not likely that for every betrothal there will be a breakfast and a sending out of cake. If the occasion arises, and such an order be obtained, the practical man will doubtless rise to the occasion.

ILLUSTRATIONS I.-VIII., SECTION II.

SHILLING GATEAUX

THESE goods have been attracting the attention of confectioners more and more in recent years. They are, or should be, both bright and pretty. They are very saleable and enhance the general shop display. They should be made from a good Genoese base, either a light egg mixture or a closer-eating butter mixing. The latter seems to be the favourite of the English cake-eating public, and therefore we give a suitable recipe :—

> 2 lbs. Butter
>
> 2 lbs. Sugar
>
> 2 lbs. Eggs
>
> $2\frac{1}{4}$ lbs. Flour
>
> $\frac{1}{4}$ oz. Powder.

Unless when it is otherwise stated, the powder mentioned in these mixings for Gateaux is made as follows :—

> 2 lbs. Cream Tartar
>
> 1 lb. Carbonate Soda.

Mix thoroughly and pass through a fine sieve several times. Keep this powder in a dry place in an air-tight tin.

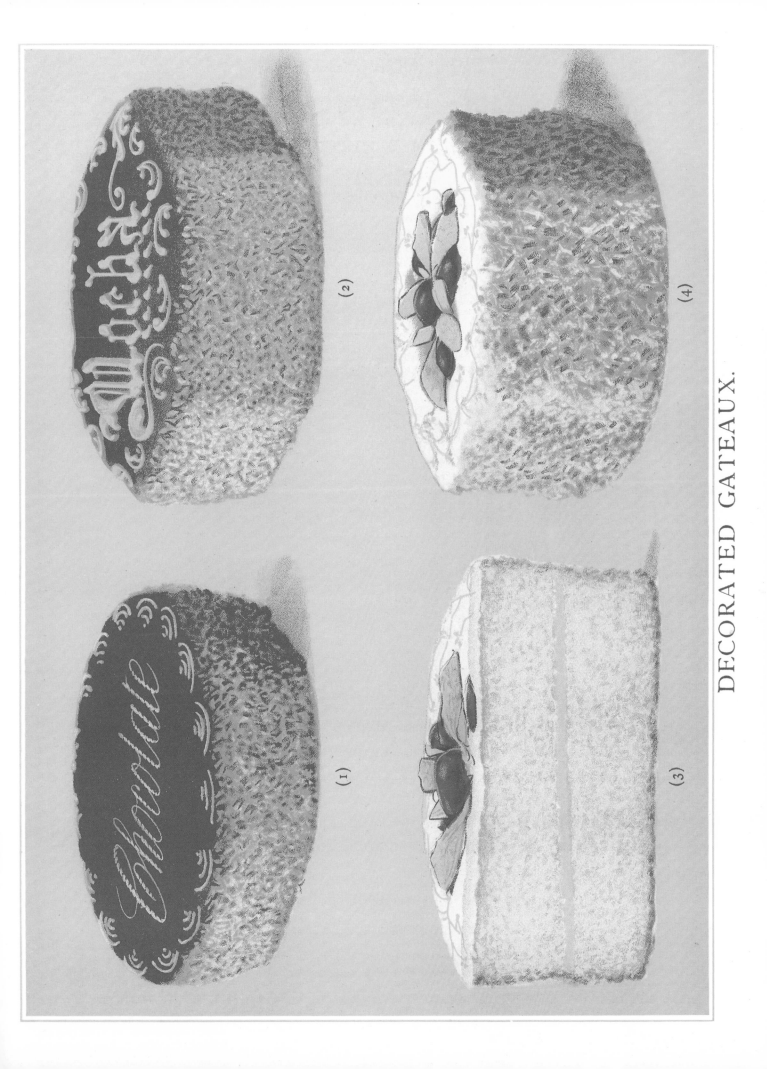

(1)   (2)   (3)   (4)

DECORATED GATEAUX.

WILLIAM COOK & SONS,
OVEN BUILDERS,
BURNSIDE, PIERSHILL, EDINBURGH.

The above is an illustration of our PATENT "MATCHLESS" STEAM HOT PLATE for baking Scones, Muffins, Crumpets, Pancakes, Oatcakes, and all Hot Plate goods. The baking heat can be regulated at will to suit any class of goods requiring either a slow or quick heat.

The heat is perfectly uniform all over the baking area, and the saving in fuel when compared with gas plates is in some cases 90%. These are Facts arrived at after independent tests made by some of our customers.

These Hot Plates are made in lengths varying from 6 ft. to 18 ft., and are all 2 ft. 6 in. wide. They are strongly and proportionately built, and will last a lifetime.

For further Particulars, Prices and Testimonials, apply to the Patentees and Sole Makers—

WILLIAM COOK & SONS, Burnside, Piershill, Edinburgh.

Cream the butter and sugar, add the eggs by beating in slowly two or three at a time, then mix in the other ingredients in the usual manner, and weigh into hoops and various fancy shaped tins, at about 10 ozs. or 12 ozs. each, according to the class of trade. Bake in a sound oven. They should not be finished off until the following day; they should then be sliced through and filled with a layer of Butter Cream prepared thus :—

1 lb. Best Butter

1 lb. Icing Sugar

Flavouring and Colouring.

Beat the butter and sugar together and flavour and colour to suit. Pink colour and strawberry flavour are used in the section shown in the illustration, and this would probably meet all requirements.

These cakes ought to be masked in really good fondant, that well covers the cake and retains a fine gloss. The sides may either be left plain or may be covered with browned cocoanut.

Some examples are given amongst which will be noticed Chocolate (1), Mocha (2), Strawberry (5), and White (6). The illustration (7), showing a round white gateau with a spray of fruits, might be priced at 1s. 6d., as it takes more fruit and time to execute.

WALNUT GATEAU

THE shilling Walnut Gateau is cut out of a sheet of Genoese made from the following :—

    1 lb. Butter

    1 lb. Sugar

    8 Eggs

    1 lb. Flour

    2 ozs. Ground Walnuts

    Pinch Powder.

Cream up butter and sugar, add eggs, flour, etc., in the usual way, and spread the mixing about 1 inch thick on a baking-sheet, taking care that it is the same thickness all over. Bake in a sound oven.

When cold, cut into squares of from 4 to 5 inches. Slice through the middle and put in a layer of butter cream. Then mask in white fondant, and pipe the lines on in pink and green icing and finish with half walnuts and silver dragees. Instead of piping the tops with coloured icing, jams and jellies of suitable appearance may be used.

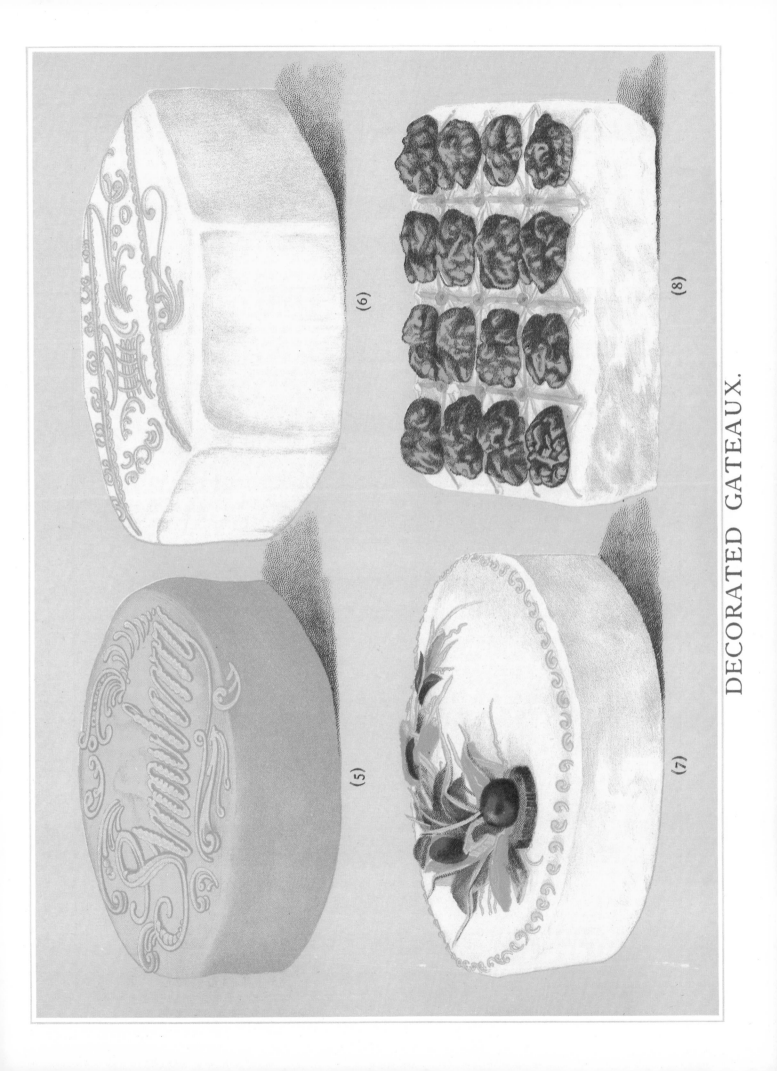

DECORATED GATEAUX.

ILLUSTRATION No. IX.

BUTTER CREAM GATEAU

THIS should not be retailed at less than 1s. 6d., but in good class shops 2s. and 2s. 6d. are the prices.

Cut out a square of ordinary Genoese of suitable size, slice through, fill with butter cream, and slightly mask tops and sides with the same.

Place some Langues de Chat biscuits in position round the sides as shown in the illustration, mark four triangular divisions on the top, and pipe on stars of two different coloured creams, such as coffee and yellow, pink and white, etc., having the same colour in two opposite spaces.

Tie a piece of ribbon, of a pale shade, round the gateau, finishing it with a pretty bow.

ILLUSTRATION No. X.

BATTENBURG CAKE

FOR this cake take a good Genoese mixing—the one given for shilling gateaux will do nicely.

Colour one portion red and leave another plain, spread each colour on a separate baking-sheet about $\frac{3}{4}$ inch thick and bake in a sound oven.

When cold, cut from the Genoese nine bars of a suitable length and about one inch wide and one inch deep. Place them together with colours alternating, as shown in the illustration, and fix with apricot jam.

Then roll out a sheet of almond paste to about $\frac{1}{4}$ inch thick, place the cake upon this, first masking it all over with jam to make it stick.

Roll the cake up in the paste, making the sides neat and flat, and hiding the join of the sheet.

This cake may either be left plain or the edges pinched or crimped as in the illustration, or the top may be coated with fondant and finished off with piping or other decoration.

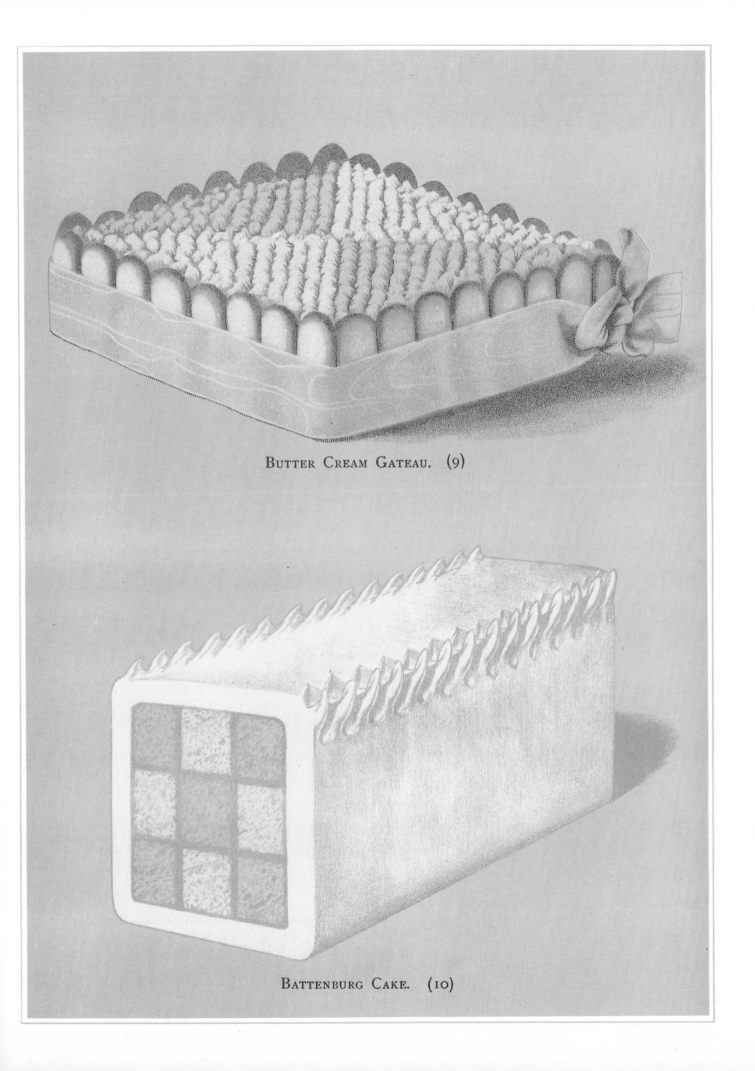

BUTTER CREAM GATEAU. (9)

BATTENBURG CAKE. (10)

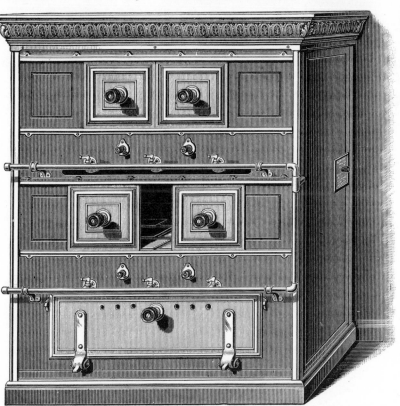

ILLUSTRATIONS Nos. XI. and XII.

MARZIPAN GATEAUX

THE price of these must be governed largely by the amount of marzipan used in the decoration. Those illustrated are retailed at from 2s. 6d. to 3s. 6d. each. The base of the cake is baked in a round hoop, in exactly the same way as those described that sell at a shilling, but the hoop should be nearly twice the size. Prepare the mixture as follows :—

> 3 lbs. Butter
>
> 3 lbs. Sugar
>
> 24 Eggs
>
> 3 lbs. Flour
>
> 6 ozs. Ground Almonds
>
> $\frac{1}{4}$ oz. Powder.

Cream the butter and sugar, beat in the eggs, and add flour, etc., in the usual manner. Weigh into the hoops about 1 lb. 2 ozs. each and bake in a moderately hot oven. When the cakes are cold, slice each through the middle and fill with butter cream, which has been coloured and flavoured to correspond with the scheme of decoration, as for example—if it is intended to use lilac or rose in the external finishing of the cake, heliotrope and rose colour and flavour must be used in the butter cream in the respective cases.   Mask each cake in white fondant and put browned chopped almonds round the sides.

The most convenient way of making the leaves is to get the prepared marzipan now sold by wholesalers and rub 1 lb. marzipan paste and 1 lb. icing sugar together on a slab until thoroughly smooth and pliable.   Break off pieces of the required size, and with the fingers mould them into the shape of leaves, and stand aside to set.

Dip each leaf in white or pale green fondant, and then, when dry, place in position on the top of the cake.   Veins should be piped on the leaves, and light piping or other decoration in keeping may be made use of.

In the case of illustration No. 11 the four lower oval-shaped leaves are masked in heliotrope and the three above in pale yellow; this constitutes a very pretty combination.   In some cases it will be found easier and better to mask the marzipan decorations after they have been placed on the cakes, and this is done by piping them with the fondant.

There are illustrated a number of very pretty cakes decorated

(11)

(12)

GATEAUX, WITH MARZIPAN LEAVES.

THE BOOK OF CAKES

"VEBERINE"

WILL KEEP FOR MONTHS.

A PURELY VEGETABLE PRODUCT.

PREPARED FROM SELECTED COCOANUTS.

WARRANTED FREE FROM ALL ANIMAL FATS.

ɤ ɤ ɤ

AN EXCELLENT SUBSTITUTE FOR BUTTER, MARGARINE, LARD, AND
OTHER FATS GENERALLY USED FOR COOKING PURPOSES.

ɤ ɤ ɤ

FREE FROM ALL PRESERVATIVES, AND, OWING TO THE
PROCESS OF MANUFACTURE, ABSOLUTELY STERILE.

WRITE FOR PRICES AND FULL PARTICULARS TO

JOSEPH CROSFIELD & SONS, Limited,
WARRINGTON.

with marzipan, and the distinction between them lies principally in the external design, the shape and colour of marzipan and other sugar work. For these better-class gateaux another method of making butter cream may be used, which, whilst taking longer to prepare, is much smoother than that previously described, besides having the useful quality of keeping comparatively soft in cold weather.

Quantities :—

> 1 lb. Loaf Sugar
>
> 1 lb. Butter (Fresh)
>
> 12 yolks Eggs
>
> Essence of Vanilla.

Cream up the butter and set aside.

Boil the sugar to the blow degree and add the yolks which have been previously whisked, put in a small quantity of essence of Vanilla. Beat till cool and then add the creamed butter.

As the majority of the following gateaux are to be made

from sheet Genoese the following is given as being a thoroughly reliable and high-class recipe :—

2 lbs. Butter

2 lbs. Sugar

2 lbs. Eggs

2 lbs. Flour

¼ lb. Ground Almonds

Pinch Powder.

Cream the butter and sugar, beat in the eggs and add the flour, etc., as usual. Spread evenly on a baking-sheet, which has been previously papered, and bake in a sound oven. When cold it may be cut into shapes and sizes as desired.

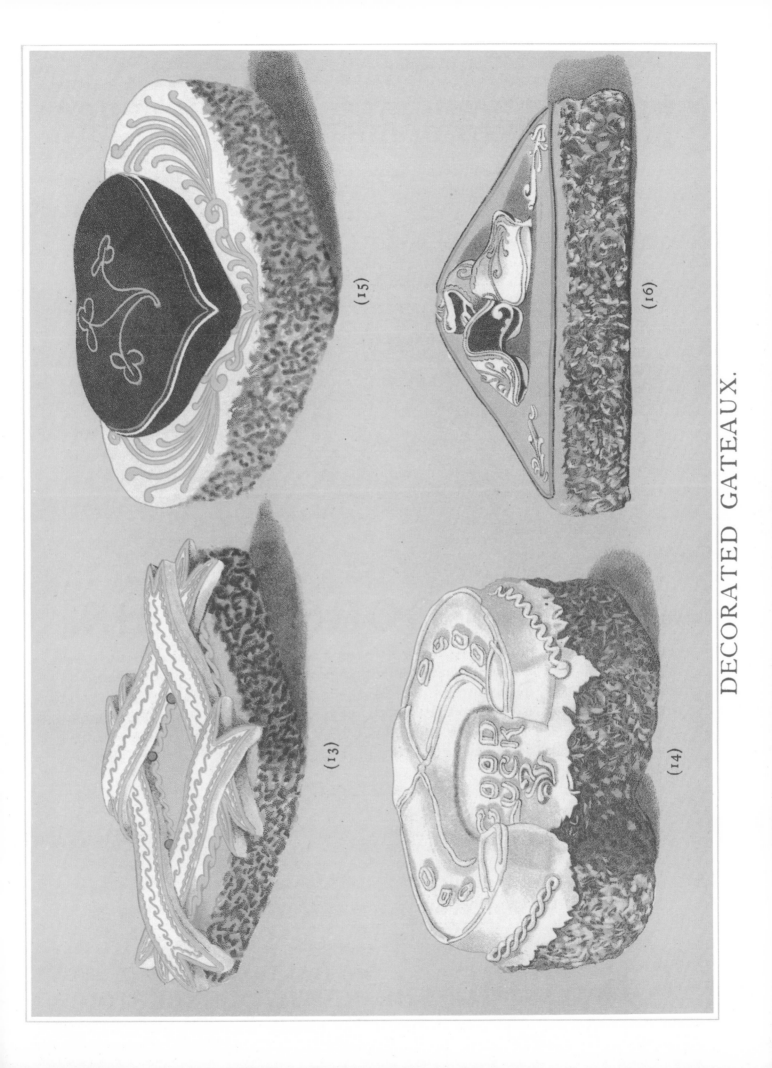

(15)

(16)

(13)

(14)

DECORATED GATEAUX.

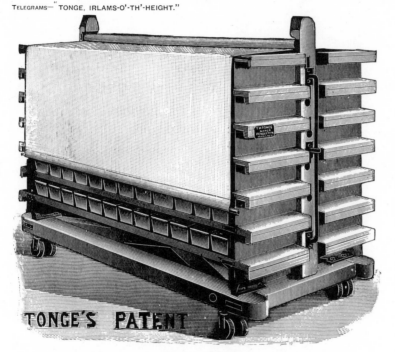

ILLUSTRATION No. XIII.

MARZIPAN GATEAU

THIS cake, which is quite simple and very effective, is cut out from a sheet of Genoese in a square shape, and is sliced through and filled with butter cream. After being spread with the cream, mask the gateau in pale pink fondant and cover the sides with brown cobbled almonds. For the top decoration, the marzipan should be rolled out in a sheet barely $\frac{1}{4}$ inch thick and cut into strips $\frac{1}{2}$ inch wide, and of suitable length. The ends are cut "swallow tail" to represent the ends of a piece of ribbon. Place four of these lengths of marzipan in position on the gateau, as shown in the illustration No. 13, one end of each strip over, and the other end under, that of another. Fill a piping bag with pale yellow fondant and cover the strips all over. When sufficiently dry, pipe a small scroll design in brown icing down the centre of each strip, and border the edges neatly.

I

ILLUSTRATION No. XIV.

HORSE-SHOE GATEAU

THE base of the single horse-shoe gateau, shown in illustration No. 14, is cut from a sheet of Genoese, and is somewhat in the shape of a horse-shoe. In this case the marzipan is put on the cake before any fondant is used. Mould the marzipan by hand into the shape of a horse-shoe and place it in the position shown. Then cover the whole cleanly and evenly in white fondant, showing the marzipan shoe clearly defined on its cake base. Cover the sides of the base with chopped almonds, and then finish by piping.

ILLUSTRATION No. XV.

HEART GATEAU

IN the cake illustrated, No. 15, the base is cut from a sheet of Genoese, in the shape of a heart. It is then masked with fondant and the sides finished with chopped browned almonds. Mould a portion of marzipan into the usually recognised shape of a heart and cover it with good chocolate fondant. Put aside on a wire to dry, and when set, place it in position on the base. With a fine tube, pipe the shamrock leaves, border, etc.

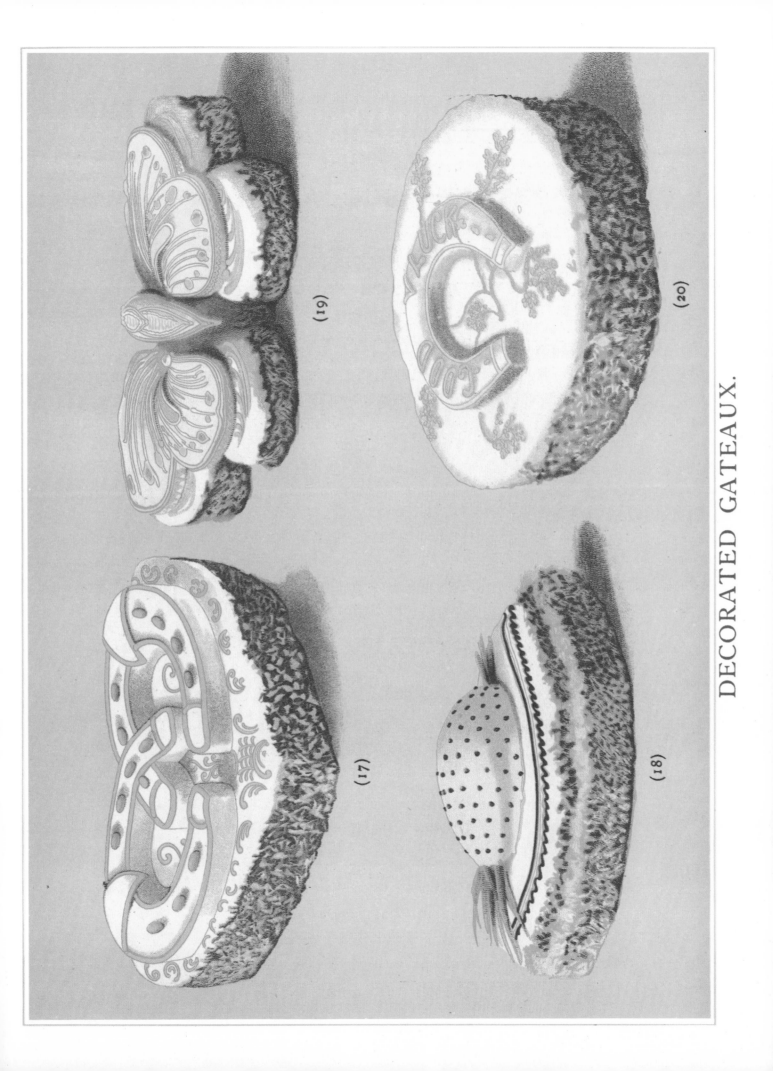

DECORATED GATEAUX.

THE BOOK OF CAKES

WERNER, PFLEIDERER & PERKINS'

PATENT

STEAMPIPE "TELESCOCAR" DRAWPLATE

and

"PERKINS" PEEL OVENS

FIRED BY COKE OR PRODUCER GAS

For all Kinds of

CAKE AND CONFECTIONERY.

**The Ovens here shown are used solely for baking
Cakes and Biscuits.**

Mixing Machines.   "Geddis" Whisks.
Bun Dividers.

Full Particulars on Application to—

43 REGENT SQUARE, GRAYS INN ROAD, LONDON, W.C.

ILLUSTRATION No. XVI.

TRIANGULAR GATEAU

CUT out a triangular piece of Genoese, and slice through the centre and fill with butter cream. Mask top and sides with fondant. The sides may be covered with brown cobbled almonds, or they may be left with plain fondant, according to taste. To make the bent scrolls on the top, first roll out a sheet of marzipan, cut some short strips of a proper width, and then bend or curl them as shown. Place in position and cover the top side of each in pale cream and the underneath in chocolate, by piping them with fondant. The borders and other decoration should be piped with pale cream and brown icings, using a fine tube.

ILLUSTRATION No. XVII.

HORSE-SHOES GATEAU

WE illustrate in No. 17 a very effective gateau with inter-twined horse-shoes.. The base is cut from a sheet of Genoese and is in the shape of a heart. It is sliced through the centre and filled with a layer of butter cream. The marzipan is moulded into two horse-shoes of equal size. One is placed in position (the left hand one in the illustration), the other must then have a small piece cut out of it to allow the end of the first to pass through; both ends should be balanced so as to give them an even appearance. Mask the whole in glossy white fondant, taking care to drain the open spaces between the shoes so as to give clear definition and to show depth. Cover the sides of the base with browned cobbled almonds and finish with fine piping.

ILLUSTRATION No. XVIII.

PINEAPPLE GATEAU

THIS gateau is made in two tiers—having the top one thinner and smaller than the lower one. Slice each tier through the centre and put in a layer of butter cream flavoured with pineapple and coloured yellow. Mask with white fondant and cover the sides with browned chopped almonds. Mould a piece of marzipan into the shape of a half pineapple and mask it carefully with yellow fondant. Stand it on a draining wire to set, and when dry, place in position on the top of the cake. Cut the angelica for the ends very thin and finish by piping the eyes of the pineapple in chocolate.

ILLUSTRATION No. XIX.

BUTTERFLY GATEAU

IN No. 19 is shown a Butterfly Gateau for which the base is cut out from a sheet of Genoese, somewhat in the shape of the wings. This can be best effected by having a cardboard pattern which is placed on the Genoese and marked round, after which it can easily be cut out. The cake is then cut through the centre to admit a layer of butter cream; it is then masked with fondant and chopped pistachio kernels are put round the sides. The body and wings of the butterfly should be formed by hand from marzipan, some little time before it is required, so that they may become surface dried. Mask them in yellow fondant and place in proper position on the base, after which they should be piped in heliotrope and pale green, getting in the lines and spots on the wings as nearly natural and correct as possible.

ILLUSTRATION No. XX.

"GOOD LUCK" GATEAU

ILLUSTRATION No. 20 shows a single horse-shoe gateau made by cutting a base from a sheet of Genoese. The shoe is moulded in marzipan and is placed in position on the base. The whole is then masked in good white fondant—taking care, as before, to drain the inside of the horse-shoe so that the moulded work may be clearly defined. The sides of the base are covered with browned almonds and the spray of maidenhair fern lightly piped on the top. This, with the outlining and printing of the words "Good Luck" on the shoe, completes the decoration of this very effective cake.

ILLUSTRATION No. XXI.

DECORATED APRICOT SPONGE CAKE

IN the illustration is shown a decorated sponge cake. The cake should be made from the following mixing:—

3 lbs. Sugar

30 Eggs

3 lbs. Flour.

Beat the sugar and eggs up in a sponge machine, lightly mix in the flour, and fill into prepared hoops of the required size and bake in a sound oven. When cold, slice the cake through, once or more, and put in one or more layers of lemon cheese curd (see recipe below). Mask the sides with warm apricot jam and cover with white desiccated cocoanut. The top, after being coated with white fondant, must be decorated with preserved fruits.

Recipe for lemon curd:—

4 lbs. Sugar

12 Lemons

1 lb. Butter

18 Eggs.

Put the butter and sugar in a large stew-pan over the fire to melt. Squeeze the juice from the lemons and add.   Thoroughly whisk up the eggs, either by hand or better in a machine, and when the butter and sugar have become well amalgamated pour in the eggs, keeping up a smart beating with a hand whisk to well mix.   The whole mixing is then kept well stirred over the fire, until it reaches a temperature of about 200 deg. Fahr., on no account allowing it to boil.

ILLUSTRATION No. XXII.

DECORATED RASPBERRY SPONGE CAKE

IN No. 22 we have another decorated sponge cake the base of which is baked in precisely the same way as No. 21.   It has to be sliced through once or twice and filled with raspberry jam. The sides are then spread with warm apricot jam and covered with white cocoanut.   The four different coloured fondants on top should be laid on with an icing bag and plain pipe, and the spaces in between piped in coffee butter cream with a star pipe.

K

ILLUSTRATIONS Nos. XXIII. and XXIV.

TWO TENNIS CAKES

THIS is a cake much in request during the summer season, and may be varied in decoration to include such games as golf, hockey, badminton, or any other popular game, during the progress of which afternoon tea is served. The cake proper should be made of some delicate mixture such as the following :—

1 lb. Butter

1 lb. Sugar

1 pt. Eggs

1 lb. 2 ozs. Flour

1 lb. Citron, cut in small cubes

$\frac{1}{2}$ lb. Currants

$\frac{1}{2}$ lb. Cherries

$\frac{1}{4}$ lb. Ground Almonds.

Cream up the butter and sugar, and add the eggs a few at a time, beating the mixing well all the time. Stir in the flour, almonds, and fruit, weigh into oblong tins of the desired size, and bake in a moderate oven. When cold, level the top if necessary by taking off a thin slice, and cover with a layer of almond paste about $\frac{1}{2}$ inch

(23)

(24)

(21)

(22)

TWO TENNIS CAKES.

DECORATED GATEAUX.

to $\frac{3}{4}$ inch thick.   The decoration should consist of a coating of white fondant (top only) and such piping, or other decoration, as may be most suitable for the purpose desired.   In illustration No. 23, the cake is finished by writing the word "Tennis" from corner to corner diagonally across the cake, the corners being filled, in the one case with chopped pistachio kernels, and in the other case by placing on a silvered tennis racquet made of papier-mâché and some light piping, with a border.   Tiny silver and gold lace edging is used on both cakes, and gives a very light, bright effect.

ILLUSTRATIONS Nos. XXV. AND XXVI.

SIMNEL CAKE

THIS cake is very popular in some parts of the kingdom, particularly at Eastertide. The writers do not claim that this is the one and only original Simnel Cake, but they offer it to their readers as a very good high–class, marketable cake which is known by the above name in most parts of the country.

RECIPE

3 lbs. Butter

3 lbs. Sugar

30 Eggs

$2\frac{3}{4}$ lbs. Flour

$1\frac{1}{2}$ lbs. Peel

5 lbs. Currants.

Cream the sugar and butter and beat the eggs in slowly in the usual way. Mix in the flour and fruit. A small quantity of this mixing is put in the bottom of each hoop and then a layer of almond paste composed as follows :—

SIMNEL CAKE. (25)

SIMNEL CAKE.—SECTION.

(26)

JOSEPH BAKER & SONS,
LIMITED.

HIGHEST AWARDS AT THE WORLD'S EXHIBITIONS

INCLUDING

34 GOLD MEDALS

FOR

BREAD AND CAKE MACHINERY,

BISCUIT MACHINERY,

PATENT CONTINUOUS BAKING OVENS.

BAKER'S NEW PATENT DECKER DRAW-PLATE CONTINUOUS BAKING OVEN.

COMPLETE MODERN BAKERY PLANTS OF ANY SIZE.

Illustrated Catalogues, etc., sent free on application.

ENGINEERS, WILLESDEN JUNCTION, LONDON, N.W.

SIMNEL CAKE 77

2¾ lbs. Almonds

3 lbs. Sugar

9 yolks of Eggs

A small quantity of Rum.

Take care that the layer of almond paste does not get nearer than
½ inch to the side of hoop. Then follows another layer of the cake
mixing, which, in finding its level, fills up the narrow space round
the outside of the almond paste and thus completely envelopes the
latter in the cake. Whilst the cake is baking, prepare a paste of

1¾ lbs. Almonds

2¼ lbs. Sugar

8 Whites of Eggs.

When the batch comes from the oven, lay this paste round the inner
edge of the top of the cake and with the aid of a fork make it
rocky. It must now be placed in a quick oven to brown, taking
care not to dry the cake, and to keep a clear space just in the centre
of the top of the cake. When cold this open space may be filled
with fondant and decorated with preserved fruits, fondant sweets,
leaves, etc. A section of this cake is shown in illustration No. 26,
which gives a good idea of how it should be finished.

SECTION III., PLATE Iᴀ

FANCY GOODS—1. CHERRY CAKES

ON plate 1ᴀ is shown a good collection of penny and twopenny fancy goods. Commencing at the top left hand illustration we have a Sponge Cherry Cake (No. 1). Prepare three dozen medium-sized, rather flat patty pans by well cleaning, greasing and dusting out with flour.

Knock up the following mixture in a machine or in a bowl :—

1 lb. Eggs

14 ozs. Sugar

14 ozs. Flour.

When the batter is ready, stir in the flour and lay out with a Savoy bag into the pans. Bake and turn out. Cover the sides with apricot jam, coloured pink, and roll in desiccated cokernut. Ice the top with fondant or water icing and place a half cherry in the middle.

(1) CHERRY CAKES.

(2) PRESSBURGS.

(3) CHERRY STRIPS.

(4) GINGER CAKES.

(5) MADELINES.

(6) ENGLANDERS.

(7) VIENNESE STRIPS.

(8) TURK'S CAPS.

(9) ALMOND SLICES.

(10) POMMES DE TERRE.

(11) CREAM BASKETS.

(12) CAFÉ CAKES.

(13) MADEIRA TARTLETS.

(14) PRINCE OF WALES' CAKES.

(15) SPONGE CHEESE CAKES.

(16) COCOANUT TARTLETS.

(17) MALVERNIANS.

(18) HAZELNUT. MERINGUE GENOESE.

(19) CHOCOLATE BISMARCKS.

(20) DECORATED SPONGE, FANCY.

PAGE 1A, SECTION 3.

VARIETY OF FANCY CAKES AND PASTRIES.

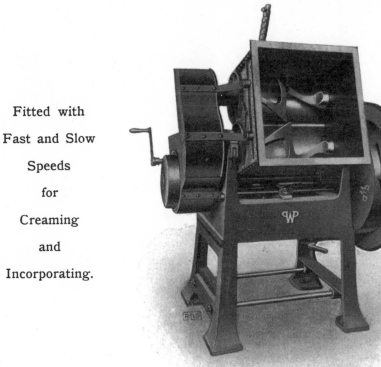

2. PRESSBURGS

CUT out from a sheet of Genoese or from a Madeira or other plain cake, some strips or fingers measuring from 2 to 3 inches long and $\frac{1}{2}$ inch thick.   Mix the following ingredients:—

6 Yolks

$\frac{1}{2}$ lb. Sugar

$\frac{1}{2}$ lb. Ground Almonds

Spread over the whole of the fingers, cover with cobbled almonds, place in the oven and bake to a nice brown colour.

3. CHERRY STRIPS

THIS is a very good line, though the illustration hardly shows it to advantage.   Make a dough of the following quantities :—

$\frac{1}{2}$ lb. Flour

6 ozs. Butter

$\frac{1}{4}$ lb. Sugar

3 ozs. Almonds

1 Yolk.

Roll out in two strips about 18 or 20 inches long and 3 inches wide, place on a baking-sheet, roll a small piece of dough into a length, and place along each edge and partly bake.   When cold, place 14 ozs. of whole cherries along the strips and cover with a mixture of

3 Eggs

4 ozs. Sugar

4 ozs. Ground Almonds.

The eggs and sugar are to be whisked together and the almonds added.   Place in the oven again and finish baking.   When cold, dredge some icing sugar over, making them quite white.   Cut into strips and sell.

4. PENNY GINGER CAKES

CLEAN some fluted cup moulds like those shown in illustration and grease them carefully. When they are quite ready and laid out on a baking-sheet, prepare the following mixing:—

10 ozs. Butter

8 ozs. Sugar

8 ozs. Syrup

1¼ lbs. Flour

½ oz. Ginger

½ oz. Spice

A little milk, in which is dissolved a pinch of Bicarbonate of Soda.

Sprinkle a few sliced almonds in the bottom of each mould and nearly fill each with the mixing. Bake in a moderate oven.

L

5. MADELINES

CAREFULLY grease out some plain Dariole moulds and set them aside on a baking-sheet. Prepare the following mixing :—

> 1 lb. Sugar
>
> 14 ozs. Butter
>
> 12 Eggs
>
> 1 lb. Flour
>
> A pinch of Powder.

Cream up the butter and sugar well, add in the eggs (a few at a time), and stir in the flour into which the pinch of powder has been carefully sifted. Fill the mould three parts full and bake in a sound oven. When cold, turn upside down and pipe a spot of fondant on each one. Finish by placing a half cherry in the centre of each spot of icing.

6. ENGLANDERS

THIS, as the name implies, is of German origin.   Take

2 lbs. Sugar

1¼ lbs. Ground Almonds,

and enough whites of eggs to make it a little tighter than the consistency for macaroons.   Spread the mixture on strips of wafer paper 3 inches wide.   Keep the mixing about ⅛ inch thick.   Sprinkle cobbled or sliced almonds over it.   Cut into penny pieces.   Let dry for awhile, and then bake in a cool oven.

7. VIENNESE STRIPS

2 lbs. Flour

1 lb. Butter

1 lb. Sugar

3 Eggs

Essence of Vanilla.

MIX to a dough, roll out a long piece about 3 inches wide and rather more than ⅛ inch thick.   Wash with egg, sprinkle chopped almonds all over and roll them in.   Then cut into penny strips.

8. TURK'S CAPS

1 lb. Butter

$1\frac{1}{4}$ lbs. Sugar

$1\frac{1}{2}$ lbs. Eggs

2 lbs. Flour

$\frac{3}{4}$ oz. Powder.

CREAM up the butter and sugar, then add the eggs, and stir in the flour as usual. Keep the mixing fairly slack; fill into upright tins and bake. When cold, cover the sides in apricot jam, then roll in desiccated cocoanut. Ice with fondant, and place a cherry on top of each cake.

9. ALMOND AND COCOANUT SLICES OR CUTS

MAKE a sweet paste—generally known as German paste—from the following quantities :—

2 lbs. Flour

1½ lbs. Butter

½ lb. Sugar

3 Eggs.

Roll out in strips about 18 inches long and 3 inches wide, place on a baking-sheet and egg-wash the edges, and run an edge of dough along. Finish this in the same way as is done with Shortbread, and partly bake.   When cool, fill with either of these mixtures :—

(1) ½ lb. Chopped Almonds

¾ lb. Sugar

6 Whites

Cinnamon.

(2) ½ lb. Cocoanut (coarse)

¾ lb. Sugar

6 Whites

Vanilla.

Mix the ingredients of either of the above recipes in a stew-pan, and bring just to the boil over a smart fire. After this has been filled into the prepared paste, bake in a quick oven, and then cut into strips.

10. POMMES DE TERRE

ROLL out a sheet of marzipan about ⅛ inch thick and cut into oblong shapes. Cut out some suitable sized pieces of Genoese, rather oblong in shape. Dip these into syrup flavoured with rum, and place one piece on each square of paste. Fold the marzipan in such a manner as to cover the Genoese, forming it to the usual shape of a potato. Roll in chocolate powder to give it an earthy appearance, and with a pointed stick stab small holes to represent the eyes.

11. CREAM BASKET

MAKE some sweet paste as for the Almond Cuts. Line some fluted basket-shaped pans with it and bake. Fill, when cold, with whipped cream or boiled meringue. Cut out the lids from a sheet of Genoese and place in position. The handle is formed with a stick of angelica.

12. CAFÉ CAKE

MAKE a sponge mixture as follows:—

36 Eggs

3 lbs. Sugar

3 lbs. Flour.

Whisk up the eggs and sugar, and lightly stir in the flour. With the flour stir in $\frac{3}{4}$ lb. butter, melted on the oven stock. Spread the mixing on a baking-sheet and bake. When cold, cut into squares and oblongs, and, placing them together closely on a baking-sheet, spread them with—

1 lb. Sugar Nibs

1 lb. Chopped Almonds

Sufficient yolks to make the other ingredients stick.

Put them in a quick oven to get nicely coloured, and then with a knife carefully separate each cake where it has been previously cut.

13. MADEIRA TARTLETS

LINE some fine fluted cup pans with German paste made by mixing—

> 1 lb. Flour
>
> $\frac{3}{4}$ lb. Butter
>
> $\frac{1}{2}$ lb. Sugar
>
> 2 Eggs.

When ready, fill each mould with the following:

> 1 lb. Sugar
>
> 1 lb. Butter
>
> 12 Eggs
>
> 1 lb. Flour,

and bake in a sound oven.

14. PRINCE OF WALES' CAKES

2 lbs. Butter

2½ lbs. Sugar

3 lbs. Eggs (in shell)

4 lbs. Flour

1 oz. Mixed Powder.

THE powder is in the proportion of two parts of cream of tartar to one of soda. Rub out and grease a number of deep fluted pans. Cream the butter and sugar, adding the eggs gradually, stir in the flour, fill into the pans, and bake. They can either be left plain or a cherry can be placed on top as shown.

15. SPONGE CHEESE CAKES

THESE should be made when making sponges or other sponge fancies. Small patty pans should be lined with a thin sheet of puff paste, cut out with a fluted cutter. Fill these with the finished mixing and bake. When cold, ice the tops neatly with fondant.

M

16. COCOANUT TARTLETS

LINE the fine fluted pans as in No. 13. Fill with the following mixing and bake:—

2 lbs. Sugar

1 lb. Cocoanut

12 Whites.

Give this a thorough beating before filling into the pans.

17. MALVERNIANS

PREPARE some deep, plain round pans by greasing and dusting out with flour and sugar. Knock up the following mixture:—

$2\frac{1}{2}$ lbs. Eggs

$2\frac{1}{4}$ lbs. Sugar

$2\frac{1}{4}$ lbs. Flour

6 ozs. of Melted Butter.

Beat up the eggs and sugar, stir in the flour lightly, and then the butter. Fill into the pans and bake. When cold, cover the sides with apricot purée—either plain or coloured pink—roll in cocoanut, ice the top with fondant, and decorate with cherries and angelica.

18. HAZELNUT MERINGUE FANCY CAKES

CUT out the base with a round cutter from a sheet of plain or Hazelnut Genoese. The top is formed of a round meringue shell, which can be made in the usual way, but round instead of egg shaped. Fill the shells with the following :—

4 Whites

$\frac{1}{2}$ lb. Sugar

$\frac{1}{4}$ lb. Ground Hazelnuts.

Knock up the whites to a snow, add the sugar and nuts. Place the shell in position on the Genoese and cover with white fondant. Decorate with blanched hazelnuts or other decoration.

19. CHOCOLATE BISMARCKS

THIS is something similar to the foregoing article, except that in this case the Genoese, etc., is of the chocolate variety. For the chocolate Genoese take :—

> 1 lb. Butter
>
> $1\frac{1}{2}$ lbs. Sugar
>
> 10 Yolks
>
> 10 Whites
>
> $\frac{1}{2}$ lb. Flour.

Cream up the butter, sugar, and yolks; whisk up the whites to a snow and add to the batter, stir in the flour, and bake on prepared baking-sheet. Cut out the base as before, but, in this instance, fill the shells with chocolate meringue made by adding a little melted block chocolate to the ordinary meringue. Cover with chocolate fondant and decorate with crystallised violets.

20. DECORATED SPONGE

PREPARE some pans about 3 inches long and $1\frac{1}{4}$ inches broad Fill with the mixture given for Malvernians and bake. When cold, ice the top with fondant and decorate with cherry and angelica.

PLATE II.

DECORATED GENOESE

ON plate 2 is shown a fine display of penny and twopenny decorated Genoese. Take Nos. 1 to 8 first. The squares, rounds, oblongs, triangles, or other shapes, are cut from the sheet of Genoese and sandwiched through the centre with preserve. The tops are then iced neatly and cleanly with white, pink, and chocolate fondant. The sides are masked in apricot purée, and covered with browned cocoanut, and then decorated with cherries and angelica.

Nos. 9 and 10 should be retailed at twopence each. Cut a rather wide strip of Genoese; slice through and put on a layer of marzipan, either white or coloured pale green, yellow or pink; use a little apricot jam to make it adhere to the Genoese. Ice the top in suitable coloured fondant to match the marzipan, cut into squares, diamonds, triangles, etc., and place a cherry on top.

In the examples Nos. 11 and 12, strips of various coloured marzipan are rolled out under the hands and then placed in position on top of a strip of Genoese, which has first been spread lightly with apricot jam. The whole is then covered with good fondant by pouring it over, and, when set, cut into penny or twopenny pieces.

SECTION III., PLATE III.

Nos. 1 and 2 on plate 3 are simple. Cut out a strip of Genoese about 3 inches wide, slice through and jam; then cover with chocolate or other fondant, cut into neat pieces and place a half cherry and two leaves of angelica on top.

For Nos. 3 and 4 cut out a strip of Genoese about 2 inches wide, and jam through the centre. Then spread a layer of meringue on the top and dust over with icing sugar, mark into sections, place in the mouth of the oven to take on a nice brown colour; cut into pieces through the marks previously made and fix a crystallised violet on top.

In the case of Nos. 5 and 6, cut out a strip of Genoese from 2 to 3 inches wide, slice through and spread rather thickly with pink butter cream. Cover the top in the same manner, cut into penny pieces and pipe with the cream.

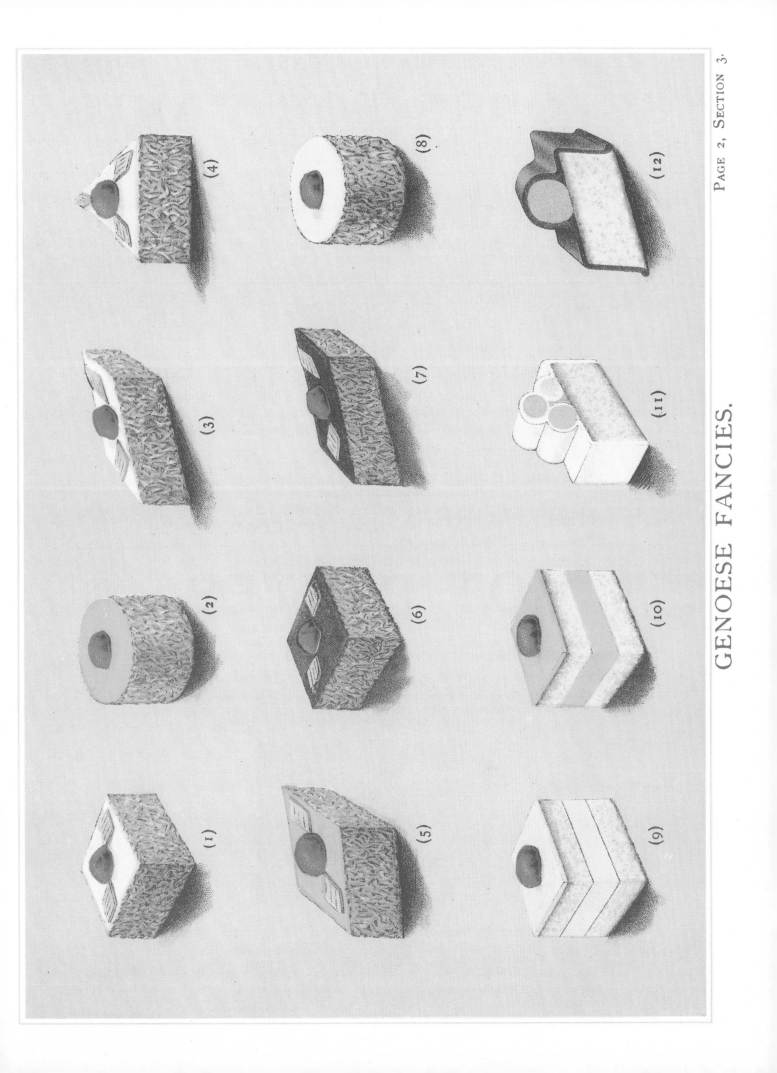

GENOESE FANCIES.

COLOURS FOR CAKES

The delicate colours shown in the illustrations of Cakes appearing in "The Book of Cakes" can be secured by using

MORRIS'S ICING COLOURS

which are specially prepared for Ornamental work. Their brilliance and richness render the goods strikingly attractive. They are economical in use, stand acid and do not fade.

MADE IN THE FOLLOWING SHADES—

ICING FRENCH PINK.	ICING ORANGE.	ICING LAVENDER.
ICING SALMON.	ICING CHOCOLATE.	ICING RUBY PINK.
ICING GREEN.	ICING CARMINE.	ICING APRICOT.
ICING BLUE.	ICING PRIMROSE.	ICING BROWN.

Sold in Tins, 2s. 9d. and 5s. 6d. each.

ICING WHITE OF EGG FOR PIPING

Morris's Icing Composition is preferred by the best workmen before Fresh Whites, as it has more stiffening and hardening power, and comes out at half the cost of any other Icing Composition.

Tins (with Directions) at 2s. 9d. and 5s. 6d. each and upwards.

THE ORIGINAL EGG YELLOW

First Introduced 1885, and Used by the Principal Cake Makers ever since.

GEORGE MORRIS, The Confectioners' Colourman, 256 CITY ROAD, LONDON.

IMPROVED PATENT WATER

THE LATEST. # HOT PLATES. *THE LATEST.*

Made in sizes from 6 ft. to 20 ft. long by 2 ft. 6 in. broad.

SMALL FURNACE HEATED BY COKE.   NO COVERS, NO ARCHES TO GIVE WAY.
HEAT EQUALLY DISTRIBUTED.   NO FUMES, PERFECT CLEANLINESS.

Can be worked a full day for from 4d. to 6d. worth of fuel.

One damper only required to regulate the heat. No flues to choke. Bakes all classes of hot plate goods to perfection. Steady baking. These Plates are rapidly being adopted, orders being on hand for many leading houses.

Scotch Furnace,

Steam, Hot Air

and

Drawplate Ovens.

Bakery Fittings,

and Utensils

of all kinds

supplied.

FULL INFORMATION, PRICES, AND REFERENCES FROM

JAMES CRUICKSHANK, Oven Builder and Bakery Fitter, TORPHICHEN STREET, EDINBURGH.

TELEPHONE: 877.   TELEGRAM : "OVENS, EDINBURGH."

No. 7 is treated in the same way as far as covering the top with cream. Then take the brown part off the top of the odd pieces of Genoese and chop it into small flaky pieces and place on top. Make this white by completely covering with icing sugar sifted through a muslin bag.

Examples 8, 9, 10. First cut out the pieces of Genoese to the required shapes and jam through the centre. Make a good meringue mixture (see page 51), and with a large star pipe lay out some fancy shapes on top of some; on others lay out the mixture in the shape of various fruits with a plain tube. Dry in the drying cupboard, or in a cool oven; colour the fruits slightly with carmine, so that it will show through to represent the blush, and cover with white or pale yellow fondant.

Nos. 11 and 12 are done in the same way, but a biscuit base being used in place of the Genoese. These can be made as follows :—

2 lbs. Flour

1½ lbs. Butter

1 lb. Sugar

4 Eggs.

Rub the butter in the flour, make a bay, put in the sugar and eggs, and mix. Cut out with crinkled cutter and bake. When cold, lay out the fruits and proceed as before. The stems are formed of angelica, and the eyes are piped with chocolate.

In No. 13 the meringue is piped on with a medium-sized plain tube in the shape of a pyramid, large at the base and going off in layers to a point at the top. The layers are made by making a rest in the pressure on the bag, and then starting again without lifting the tube until the top is reached. Then with a plain pipe lay a line of meringue round from the top to the bottom, spirally. Dust over with castor sugar and dry.

No. 14 is laid out in exactly the same way; but, after drying, it is dipped to the base of the pyramid in pink fondant, and then half way in chocolate.

For No. 15 lay out the six small points with a medium-sized tube in white meringue. Colour a small portion pink and lay a thin line round the points as shown, then with a wet finger flatten the top of each pyramid and place in the prover to dry. When dry, pipe three different coloured apricot jam on the points.

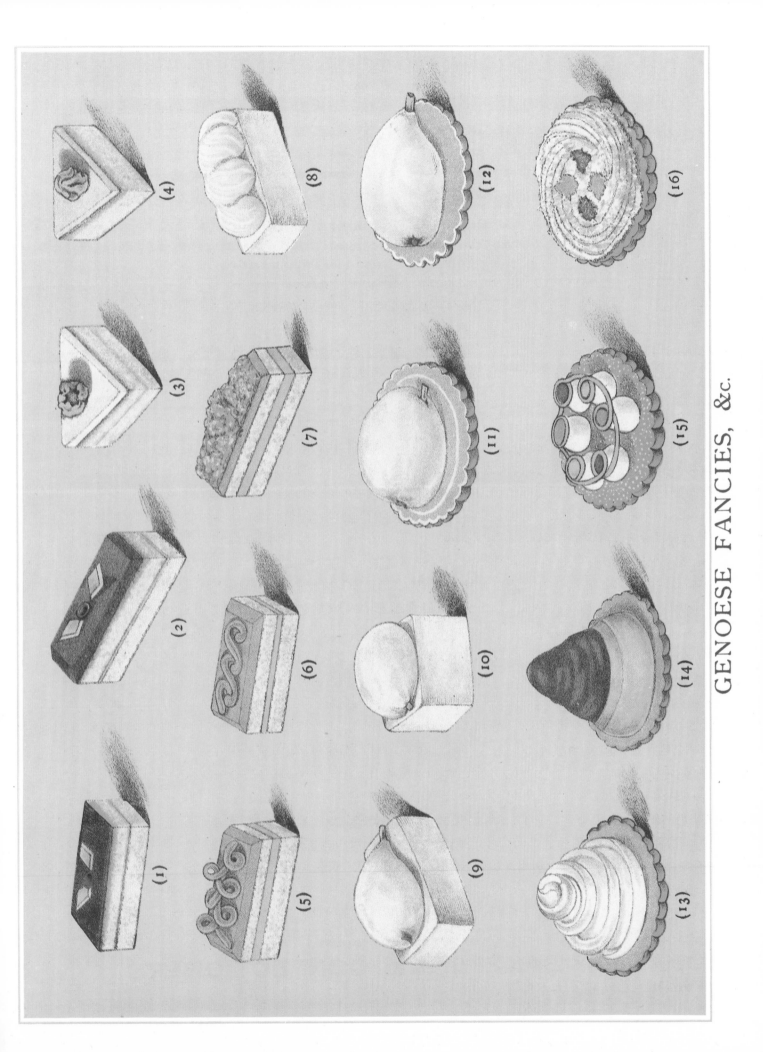

GENOESE FANCIES, &c.

Example 16. Pipe a ring of meringue round on top of the biscuit, using a large star tube; pipe a plain cross in the centre, leaving four spaces; cover with desiccated cocoanut and bake lightly. Then fill the four spaces with apricot jam, two plain and two coloured pink.

SECTION III., PLATE IV.

1. STRAWBERRY TURNOVERS

ROLL out a sheet of puff paste, cut out with a round cutter; roll a little to make it slightly longer, being thicker at the two ends and thin in the middle. Place some strawberry preserve in the centre and fold over. Wash with white of egg, dredge over with castor sugar, and bake.

2. CASTANIANS

16 Whites

14 ozs. Sugar

9 ozs. Ground Hazelnuts

5 ozs. Flour

WHISK up the whites, adding the sugar, then stir in the ground nuts and flour. Pipe out on greased tins dusted with flour, as rather large drops, and half the mixing in rings of the same size as the drops. Dust over with icing sugar and bake in a cool oven. When cold, spread the bottom of the drop with a thin layer of butter cream, place on the ring, and pipe a curl of pink cream on top with a star pipe.

3. PETIT CHOUX

$\frac{1}{2}$ lb. Butter

1 pint Water

12 ozs. Flour

10 Eggs.

PLACE the butter and water in a stew-pan on the fire and allow to boil; then shoot in the sifted flour and stir thoroughly till the mixing leaves the sides of the pan clean. Then beat in the eggs with a wooden spoon, two at a time, and work it well; lay out on tins to the required size and bake. When cold, fill with whipped cream and dip the tops in various coloured fondant.

4. CUSTARDS

THESE hardly come under the heading of fancy goods, but as they are included in the illustrations, we will give a method of making. Cut out of a sheet of puff paste a number of pieces, with a medium-sized fluted cutter.

With a smaller cutter mark out the centres, taking care not to cut right through. Put in this marked centre a paste dummy and bake. When done, remove the dummies and fill with thick custard piped from a bag.

To make this custard the following quantities are required :—

1 pint Milk

4 ozs. Sugar

1 oz. Corn-flour

3 Eggs (yolks only)

Essence of Vanilla or other flavour.

Mix the corn-flour with a little of the milk, and when smooth add the yolks and sugar and flavour. Put the remainder of the milk on the fire to boil, and when it boils pour in the corn-flour mixture and, stirring continually, bring to the boil once more, and keep boiling until sufficiently thick.

5. CHOUX FANCIES

THESE are made from the same mixture and in the same way as the Petit Choux, except that they are laid out in horse-shoe shape.   Cover the tops with pink fondant.

6. CORNUCOPIA

THESE are usually made from puff paste or puff cuttings, or a mixture of puff and short paste rolled together.   Roll out the paste and cut into long strips, wide at one end and thin at the other; and roll round the cornucopia mould by holding the mould in the right hand and twisting it round till covered with the paste. Wash and dredge with sugar, and allow to stand before baking.   When baked and cold, put in a little preserve, and then fill up with whipped cream.

7. CREAM BISCUITS

2 lbs. Flour

1 lb. Butter

$\frac{3}{4}$ lb. Sugar

4 Eggs.

MIX into a biscuit dough, roll out to about $\frac{1}{8}$ inch and cut into strips about 3 inches long by 1 inch wide, place on tins and bake; when cold, sandwich them together with the following:—

$\frac{1}{2}$ lb. Sugar (boiled)

$\frac{1}{2}$ lb. Butter

4 Yolks

1 oz. Chocolate.

Boil the sugar to the blow degree and pour on beaten yolks, When cold, add to the butter which has previously been creamed; add the chocolate melted, and a little Vanilla Essence. Cover the tops with various coloured fondant.

8. CHOUX FANCIES

THESE are made in the same way as described for No. 5, except that they are masked in chocolate fondant instead of pink.

9. ECLAIRS

TAKE the same mixing and proceed in the manner described for Petit Choux, but lay out in long finger shapes on tins and bake. When cold, cut open with the point of a knife, fill with whipped cream, and cover with chocolate or coffee fondant.

10. CREAM VICTORIAS

MAKE a sponge mixture (previously given) and bake in Victoria sandwich pans. When cold, sandwich together with the cream given for cream biscuits, but minus the chocolate. Cover the top with apricot purée, coloured pink, with a little gelatine dissolved in it, to cause it to just set; cut into triangular pieces and sprinkle chopped pistachio kernels on the ends as shown.

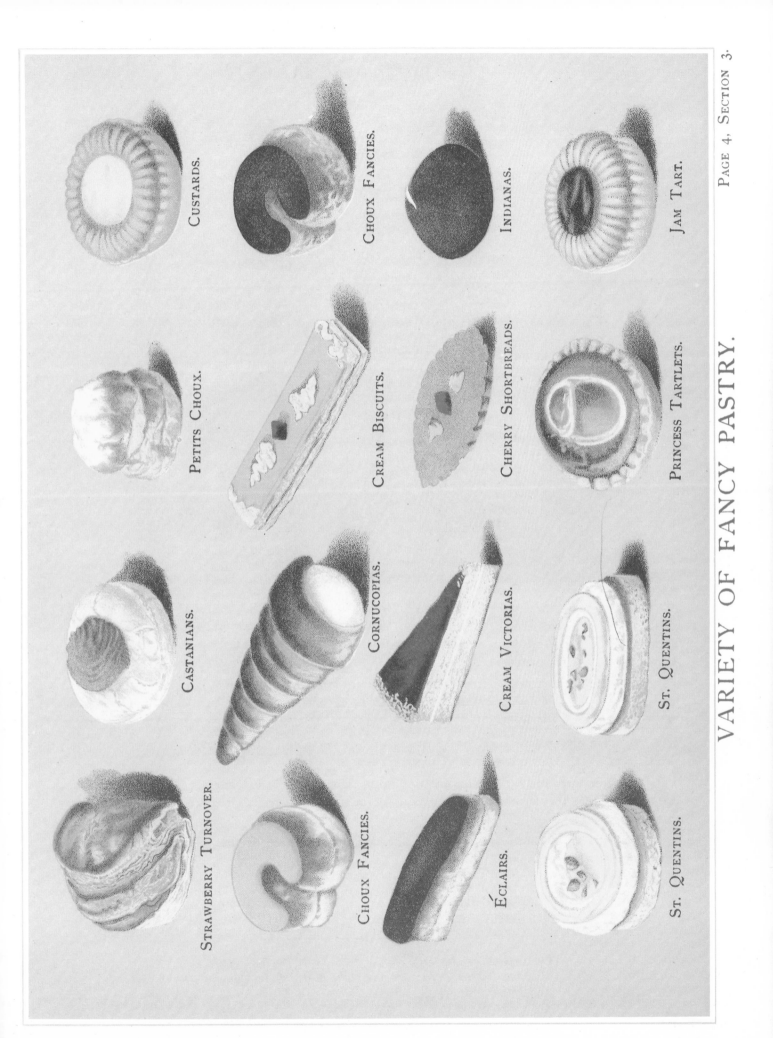

CUSTARDS.

CHOUX FANCIES.

INDIANAS.

JAM TART.

PETITS CHOUX.

CREAM BISCUITS.

CHERRY SHORTBREADS.

PRINCESS TARTLETS.

CASTANIANS.

CORNUCOPIAS.

CREAM VICTORIAS.

ST. QUENTINS.

STRAWBERRY TURNOVER.

CHOUX FANCIES.

ÉCLAIRS.

ST. QUENTINS.

VARIETY OF FANCY PASTRY.

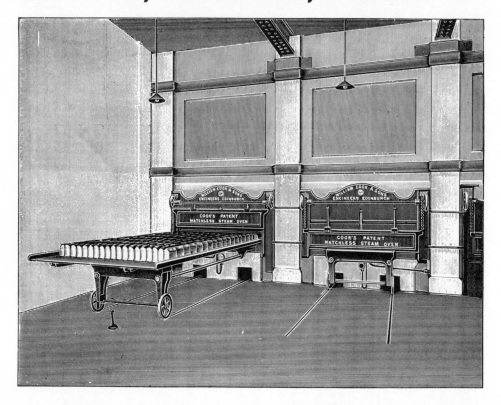

11. CHERRY SHORTBREADS

2 lbs. Flour

$1\frac{1}{4}$ lbs. Butter

1 lb. Sugar

3 Eggs.

MIX into a dough, roll to a sheet of $\frac{1}{8}$ inch thickness, and cut out with a crimped oval cutter, and bake. When cool, cover the top completely with pink fondant flavoured with essence of cherry, and place half a cherry on top.

CHOCOLATE INDIANAS

18 Whites

9 Yolks

6 ozs. Sugar

12 ozs. Flour.

KNOCK up the yolks and the sugar well with whisk. Then beat up the whites in a separate bowl, and add to the yolks; stir in lightly with a spoon and add the flour. Pipe out on greased and floured baking-sheets in bold drops, and bake in a good oven. When required to be finished off, cut out the centres and fill either with a good butter cream or custard, stick two together and mask with chocolate fondant.

13, 14. ST QUENTINS

$1\frac{1}{2}$ lbs. Flour

1 lb. Butter

$\frac{1}{2}$ lb. Sugar

3 Yolks.

MOULD the butter, sugar, and yolks into the flour, forming a nice dough, roll out rather thick, and cut out with round and oval cutters, and bake a light golden colour.

Take—

6 Whites

1 lb. Lump Sugar.

Boil the sugar to the blow, whisk up the whites, pour in the boiling syrup gradually, stirring all the time. Pipe in rings on top of the biscuits, using a large tube; colour some of the mixture a pale yellow; pipe some in the centre, and a fine ring on top of the large one. Sprinkle some chopped pistachio kernels in the centre.

15. PRINCESS TARTLETS

LINE some deep fluted pans with sweet or German paste—

> 2 lbs. Flour
>
> $1\frac{1}{2}$ lbs. Butter
>
> $\frac{1}{2}$ lb. Sugar
>
> 3 Eggs,

and fill with the following mixture:—

> 1 lb. Butter
>
> $1\frac{1}{4}$ lbs. Sugar
>
> $1\frac{1}{2}$ lbs. Eggs
>
> 2 lbs. Flour
>
> A pinch of powder.

Cream up the butter and sugar, adding the eggs gradually, and then the sifted flour; add a drop of milk, if necessary, and fill into the cases, and bake. They are either left plain or a small piece of peel is placed on top, or they are piped with meringue.

o

16. TARTLET

AS in No. 4 this is hardly a "fancy." Cut out from a sheet of puff paste a number of pieces, with either plain or fluted round cutters. Mark out the centres with a smaller cutter, and bake either with jam in, or with dummies. If baked without preserve, the tartlets may be finished by piping warm, sieved apricot, or greengage jam, or apple jelly, in sufficient quantity to fill up the space occupied by the dummies.

SECTION III., PLATE V.

1. FLORENCE TARTLET

LINE some deep pans with sweet paste, cut out with a crimped cutter, and put in a spoonful of the following cheese-cake filling :—

$\frac{1}{4}$ lb. Butter

$\frac{1}{4}$ lb. Sugar

3 Eggs

$\frac{1}{4}$ lb. Cake-crumbs.

Cream the butter and sugar, and add the other ingredients, fill into the cases, and bake. Place a little preserve on, and then pipe some meringue on top. Colour some of the latter pink, and pipe a fine line round at the top.

2. GENOESE FANCY

CUT out a strip of Genoese about 3 inches wide, slice through and spread with apricot preserve. Cover the middle of the surface in pale green fondant, leaving $\frac{1}{2}$ inch of each edge bare; afterwards cover this margin with pale yellow fondant. Pipe two lines of chocolate icing to hide the joins, and two lines of pink preserve between two fine lines of chocolate. Cut into strips about an inch wide.

3. GENOESE FANCY

CUT a strip of Genoese about 3 inches wide, slice and fill with apricot purée, coloured pink and flavoured with rum. Ice the top in pale yellow fondant and cut into narrow triangular pieces; pipe the lines, etc., finely in chocolate, and place a small piece of preserved fruit, such as a coloured pear, at the base.

4. APRICOTINES

7 Yolks

6 Eggs

8 ozs. Sugar

7 ozs. Flour.

WHISK up the sugar and eggs warm, and beat until cold; add the flour, and pipe out as drops on paper, and bake. Stick together with apricot preserve; they can either be left plain, or iced on top with fondant.

5. GENOESE FANCY

CUT out a strip of Genoese, 3 inches wide; cover with white fondant flavoured with Vanilla; cut into penny pieces, and pipe a bunch of grapes on top with meringue, using chocolate for the stalks.

6. GENOA TARTLET

LINE some fluted pans with sweet short crust, and fill with this mixture :—

> 6 Eggs
>
> ½ lb. Sugar
>
> ½ lb. Flour
>
> 6 ozs. Melted Butter.

Whisk up the eggs and sugar well, stir in the flour and add the melted butter. Spoon the mixture into the cases and bake in a sound oven. When cool, cover the tops with white fondant.

7. GENOESE PASTRY

A GENOESE strip cut out as before; ice with white fondant flavoured with Vanilla, then cut into penny pieces. Decorate with cherries and angelica.

8. PUNCH FANCIES

WITH a round or oval cutter cut out some pieces from a thin sheet of sponge (somewhat thinner than for Swiss Roll). Spread apricot preserve on one side of each. Now mix all the cuttings of Genoese and sponge, etc., that you may have on hand together in a bowl with some apricot jam thinned down with simple syrup and flavoured rather strongly with rum. Get it to a nice binding consistency, not so wet as to be sloppy nor too dry to crumble. Dip the cutter in a basin of water, and place one of the round pieces of sponge at the bottom, with the preserve side up; put in some of the mixture, and place another round of sponge on top and press together; then push the whole out of the cutter. Do this to all, and then ice with fondant. Place marzipan fruit on top and finish.

9. PUNCH FANCIES

CUT out a square or oblong piece of Genoese, mould some marzipan fruits and place on top. Colour the fruit with a little carmine, mask the whole in pale yellow fondant, and pipe on the stalks.

FLORENCE TARTLETS.   GENOESE FANCIES.   GENOESE FANCIES.   APRICOTINES.

GENOESE FANCIES.   GENOA TARTLETS.   GENOESE FANCIES.   PUNCH FANCIES.

PUNCH FANCIES.   MAZERINES.   PETITS FOURS.   RUSSIAN SANDWICHES.

 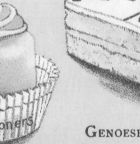 

GENOESE FANCIES.   GENOESE FANCIES.   BELFORDS.

PETITS FOURS.

VARIETY OF FANCIES.

10. MASERINES

1 lb. Flour

¾ lb. Butter

½ lb. Sugar

¼ lb. Ground Almonds

¼ lb. Cake-crumbs

2 Eggs.

FORM into a dough, and roll out a strip about ⅛ inch thick and 3 inches wide, and place on a baking-sheet; roll out a length of dough and place along the edges and partly bake, then fill with the following mixture:—

1 lb. Sugar

6 Whites

6 ozs. Almonds

Chocolate to colour.

Knock up the whites, add the sugar, stir in the almonds (chopped coarse) and the melted chocolate, and place on the fire in a bowl, keeping it continually stirred, and allow it to boil. Spread some preserve along the strips, and place this mixture on top and bake. When cold, cut into strips.

11. PETIT FOUR GLACÉ

(For instructions regarding these goods, the reader is referred to page 115.)

12. RUSSIAN SANDWICH

BAKE a thin sheet of sponge, cut in halves and place one on a clean flat baking-sheet, or in a wooden frame specially kept for the purpose.   Spread preserve on each half of the sheet.   Mix in a bowl all the cuttings of Genoese (white, pink, and chocolate) with apricot purée and syrup, flavoured with rum.   Make it to a good binding consistency, and place on the sheet on the tin; smooth over, and place the remaining half of the sheet on top, jam side down-wards; put a board on the whole with weights, and allow to stand for some hours.

When required to be finished, trim off, and cut into strips from $2\frac{1}{2}$ inches to 3 inches wide, and ice with thin and cool fondant. Have ready some cornets containing various other coloured fondant, and quickly pipe these in lines along the strips.   Drag a knife across these lines in opposite directions, giving the effect shown in the illustration.

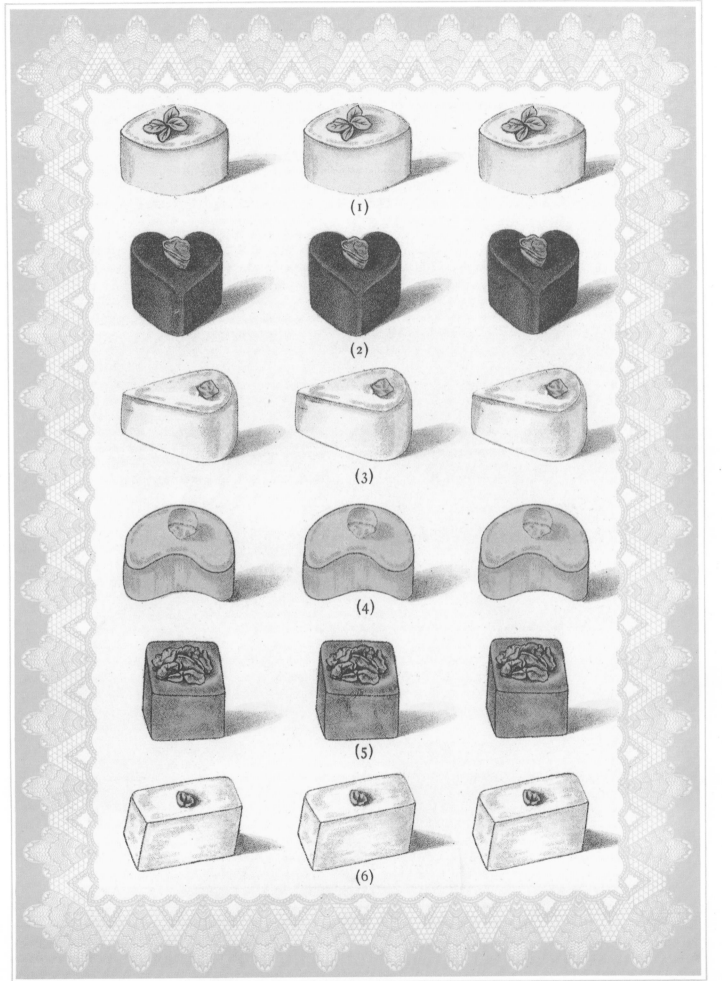

PETITS FOURS GLACES.

13. GENOESE FANCY

CUT out a strip of Genoese 3 inches wide, slice through and fill with apricot preserve; replace the top and again spread with the preserve. Roll out a sheet of almond paste or marzipan coloured yellow, about $\frac{1}{8}$ inch thick; cut into a strip of the same width as the Genoese and place on top. Cut into strips about 1 inch wide.

14. PETIT FOUR GLACE

(For particulars of making Petit Four Glacé, the reader is referred to page 115.)

15. GENOESE FANCY

CUT out a strip of Genoese $2\frac{1}{2}$ inches wide, slice through, and put a layer of marzipan through the centre. Cover the top with white fondant, and cut into strips 1 inch wide, and pipe as Dominoes with chocolate icing.

P

16. BELFORDS

THIS is a very useful cake or, perhaps, biscuit, and is quite easy to make.   Make a paste from the following quantities :—

$1\frac{1}{2}$ lbs. Flour

1 lb. Butter

10 ozs. Sugar

2 Eggs

Pinch of Powdered Cinnamon.

Rub the butter into the flour.   Make a bay and put in the sugar, eggs, and cinnamon.   Stir up eggs, etc., and mix the whole, rubbing down under hand to a firm paste.   Roll out thin and cut out with a round cutter.   When these are baked off and cold stick two together, bottom to bottom, with fine apricot jam.   Mask the top of each with white fondant and put a little bit of cherry in the centre. These goods may be made of any size to suit requirements.

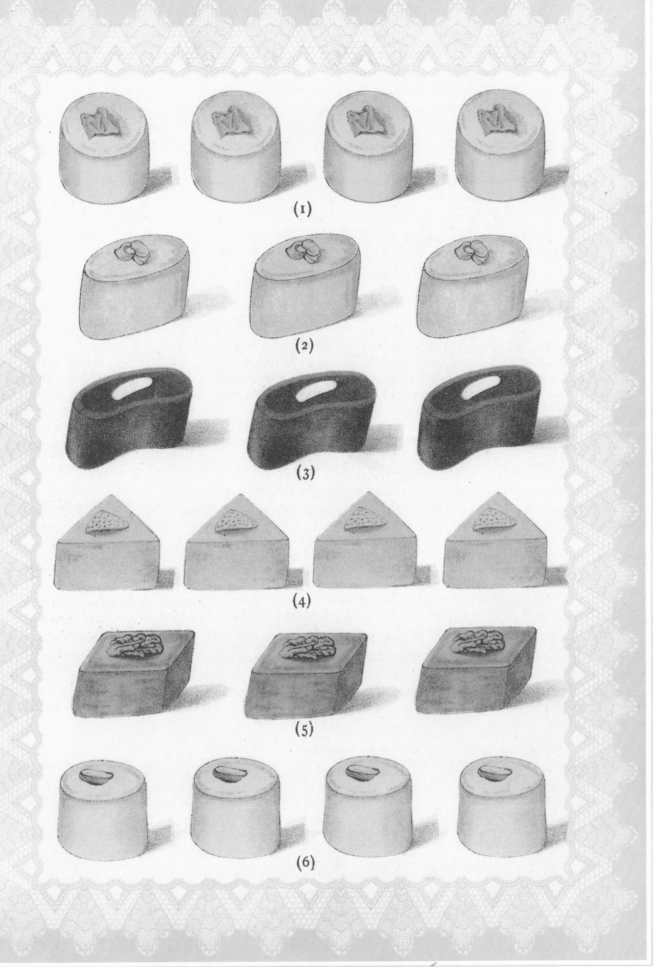

PETITS FOURS GLACÉS.

"THE BOOK OF BREAD"

IS THE

COMPANION WORK

TO

"THE BOOK OF CAKES."

By OWEN SIMMONS.

Edition de Luxe, £1, 11s. 6d.   *Ordinary Edition, 16s.*

The Illustrations

A special feature in "The Book of Bread" is the Illustrations, which are on an unparalleled scale. **Lithograph, Colour Process Work, Actual Photographs** and **Photographic Process Illustrations** have been employed in order that Volume, Colour, and Texture of the various breads illustrated may be clearly indicated. In addition to Half-Tone Illustrations in the text there are

TWENTY-TWO SEPARATE PLATES.

Representations in colours of the English and Scottish Champion Loaves are shown whole, and in section.

There are **Eight Coloured Plates** (whole loaves) representing the best loaves of different types—English, Scotch, Irish, and Welsh.

Two Beautiful Bromide Photographs of Champion Loaves are included.

The sections (crumb) of loaves will be Illustrated in the Edition de Luxe by **Eight Bromide Photographs,** and in the ordinary edition by Eight Photographic Process Illustrations of exact size.

The Photographs and Reproductions are mounted on Art Paper.

Contents

"The Book of Bread" is not overloaded with scientific terms, but is a work on Practical Bread-Making. It covers the whole field, and while it is impossible to give detailed particulars of contents, the following headings will give a fair idea of its scope. The Book is so arranged that when information is required by the reader on any particular subject or difficulty connected with the Manufacture of Bread, such information can readily be obtained.

MACLAREN & SONS, 37 and 38 SHOE LANE, LONDON, E.C.

SECTION III., PLATES VI., VII., VIII., IX.

PETITS FOURS GLACES

THESE are without doubt the smartest and prettiest after-noon fancies extant. They brighten up table, counter, or shop window, thus aiding the beauty of the whole and showing up other goods to advantage; and added to this they are a good selling line, which fact alone will commend them to most confectioners.

Great care needs to be exercised in making them as neat and "natty" as possible, as in this lies their greatest charm; nothing looks worse than an over-worked, clumsy, and perhaps highly coloured Four Glace, and yet in how many shops this variety may be seen, turned out in an unfinished manner, and presenting anything but an inviting appearance!

There seems to have arisen a question in some minds as to what is exactly meant by Petits Fours Glacés. Freely translated it means small iced cakes or biscuits, and that is precisely our conception of a description of the article with which we are now dealing. Custom has, however, fixed limitations which to a certain extent define the size, quality of cake, method and kind of icing and decoration. We say, "to a certain extent" advisedly, because competent judges are divided in opinion as to whether a fixed rule should be adhered to and a small cake masked and decorated with fondant only, made the one and only Petit Four Glacé—or whether a large margin should be allowed, and the cake covered with fondant should be piped with royal icing and decorated in any manner pleasing to the workman.

Personally we do not like these highly decorated fours glacés; there is, we think, sufficient field to make an excellent show, and to get a large variety, by the judicious use of good coloured fondant, glacé fruits, crystallised flowers, etc.

Varnish or glaze most certainly gives a showy appearance, but the good workman and the best judges like to see fondant covered goods "au naturel," with no artificial glossiness whatever. It is comparatively easy to use a poor fondant and then to highly glaze it to give it a shiny appearance, resembling to an exaggerated extent that of a well-made fondant. The glaze does not improve the eating qualities, and when, as is often the case, this glazed surface is covered with hard piping, and many silver dragees, it is still less an edible fancy cake.

The particular charm of these goods is their daintiness, and there is no other class of small confection which lends itself so completely to delicate flavouring, colouring, and decoration. Colouring especially needs great care—pale shades only should be used in nearly every case, though not so pale as to appear " washy "; the artistic workman knows what shades to use. Those who are not so gifted we advise to err on the " pale " side rather than on the " deep."

For the base it is necessary to have a good Genoese which is light without being crumbly. The following suits admirably:

2 lbs. Butter

2 lbs. Sugar

6 ozs. Ground Almonds

2 lbs. Eggs

2 lbs. Flour.

Cream up the butter, sugar, and almonds; add the eggs, a few at a time; stir in the flour; lay out on a prepared baking sheet; spread level and bake in a sound oven.

This should be made the day before it is wanted, for if cut when new the finished article will not look finished at all, owing to the crumbs of the cake becoming mixed with the fondant and giving the fours a speckled appearance which is not nice.

It must be understood that the prices to be obtained for fours glacés differs very considerably in different neighbourhoods, but the prices which may be put on goods in this article may be taken as a criterion in a fair class of trade. In the illustrations are given goods which are retailed at three prices, the first at a shilling per dozen are cut from the sheet of Genoese with a knife in squares, diamonds, triangles, strips, etc., these cause very little waste; the second are cut out in fancy shapes with cutters made for the purpose, and are sold at one and sixpence per dozen—there is a considerable amount of "cuttings" left from these;—the third are further enlarged and elaborated by the aid of marzipan and other fillings, and fetch two shillings or two and six per dozen.

We will take first these sold at one shilling per dozen.

The cost of materials employed is not great, and they should be quickly finished off—for many men make a tedious job of masking a few fancies. This is chiefly owing to not understanding the peculiar properties of fondant at various temperatures, and to not using the proper tools for working with, dipping the Genoese with forks or pouring the fondant over it with a spoon naturally takes up a lot of time. All the tools required are: small pans for melting the fondant in, with a suitable sized wooden spoon or

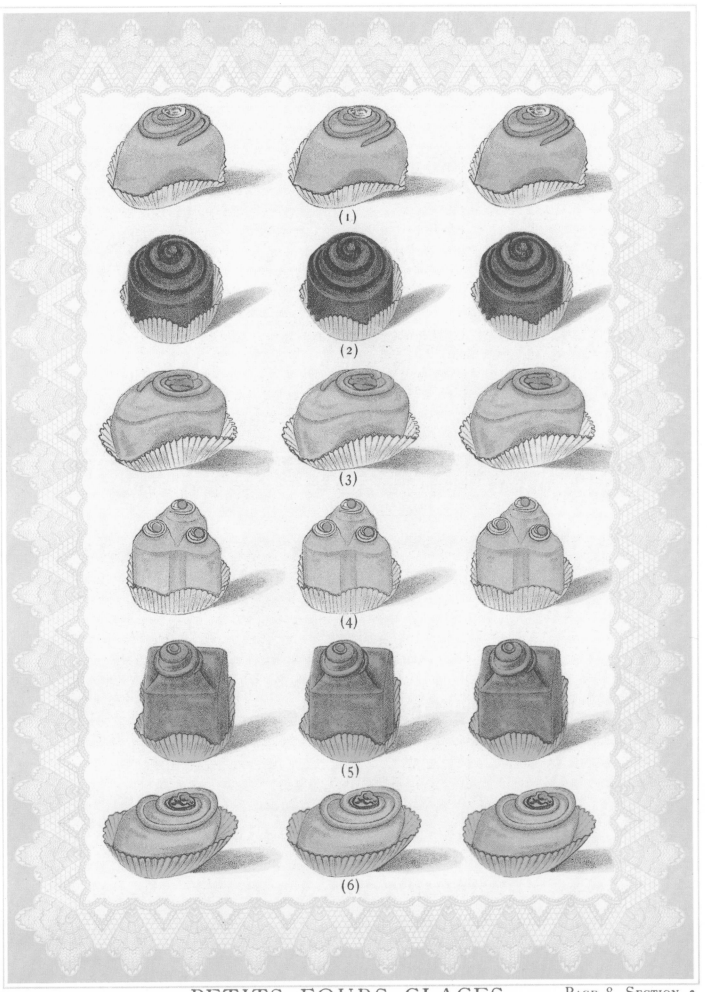

(1)

(2)

(3)

(4)

(5)

(6)

PETITS FOURS GLACES.

FRONT ELEVATION, BERMALINE BAKERY, GLASGOW INTERNATIONAL
EXHIBITION, 1901.

MODEL IN SUGAR, INDUSTRIAL HALL, GLASGOW INTERNATIONAL
EXHIBITION, 1901.

EXHIBITED AT THE BERMALINE BAKERY
AND PRESENTED BY
Messrs MONTGOMERIE & COMPANY, Limited,
TO THE CORPORATION OF GLASGOW,
AND NOW PLACED IN THE NEW ART GALLERIES.

spatula for each, and a few draining wires.   Flat tins fitted for the wire draining-trays are optional, but are very useful.

For the penny goods, cut strips from the Genoese of a suitable width, slice in two, and spread apricot preserve down the centre. Place on the top half and spread that also, and then with a sharp knife cut into the required shapes.   See Nos. 4 and 5, page 7; and Nos. 5 and 6, page 6, etc.   As already stated these being cut with a knife leave hardly any waste, whilst the remainder being pressed out with various shaped cutters, leave a considerable amount of waste which will probably have to be used up in a less profitable manner.   These latter are often cut straight out from the sheet, but if it is desired to put preserve in each, a strip should first be cut out, sliced, and preserve put in before using the cutter.   These look very pretty and are well worth a little more per dozen than the others.   See Nos. 1, 2, 3, 6, etc., plate 7.

Having cut out all the shapes required, proceed to warm up the various bowls of fondant.   The more variety of colours used, the better appearance the goods will have when laid out on trays for show, always providing that the colours are right.   Amongst those illustrated will be noticed white, yellow, orange, pale green, heliotrope, violet, coffee and chocolate.

Warm the fondant to about blood heat (this is a time-honoured phrase, but the intelligent workman soon learns the correct temperature and consistency at which to work his fondant for different goods). Place the draining wire on the tray for the purpose, or failing this, place it on the slab, put the piece of Genoese into the fondant, and take out and place on the wire tray to drain. They can either be dipped with the fingers only, or a bent piece of wire can be used for lifting out and placing on tray. A quick method is to put in one piece with the left hand, while taking out and placing in position with the right. When the draining wire is full, place it on one of the trays and put in the mouth of a cool oven for a minute or so; this will give them a fine gloss, providing they are not already set. When masking, start with the light colours and finish with the dark, otherwise smears of coffee or chocolate fondant may get on to lighter colours and spoil their appearance.

They may be finished off in a variety of ways, but for quickness and neatness we know of no better method than that adopted for these illustrations, viz. that of placing small pieces of crystallised violets, rose leaves, lilac, and fruit on the top. This is so easily and quickly done, and their appearance is so pleasing, that this style is pre-eminent. Care should be taken in the

PETITS FOURS GLACES.

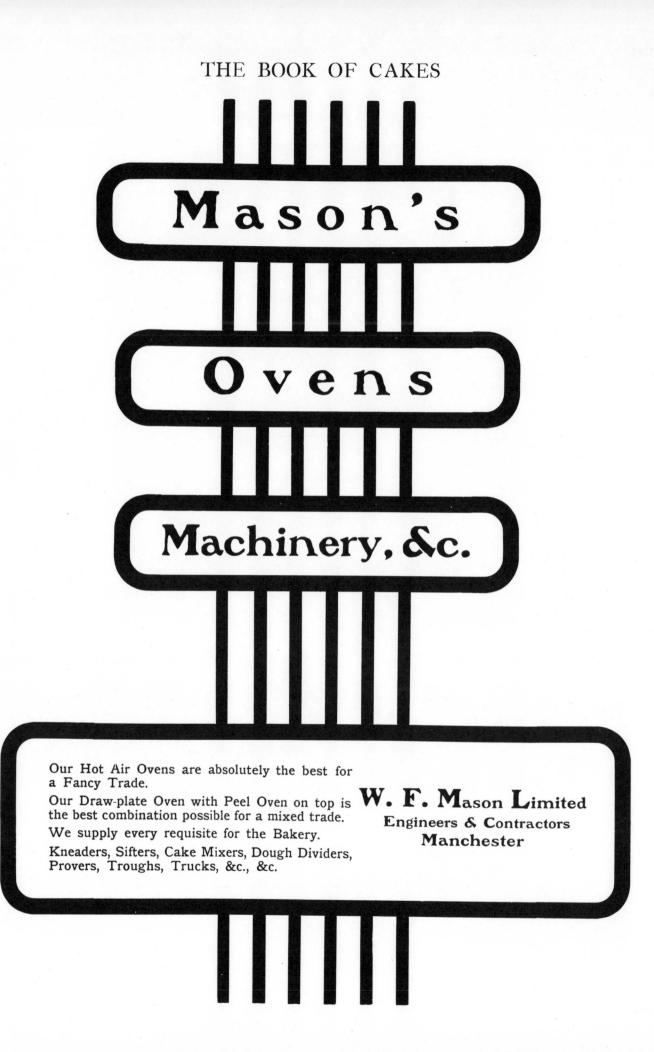

Mason's

Ovens

Machinery, &c.

selection of the right decoration, as regards colour or flavour of the fondant, thus, use glacé cherries and rose leaves on the pink, lilac on the heliotrope, violet on violet, walnuts or hazelnuts on the coffee or white, and so on. Lilac or violets look well on yellow, but walnuts on a pink ground are bad; some little taste must be exercised.

Those shown on pages 8 and 9 are raised by the addition on top of marzipan moulded to suit the shape of the cut Genoese. There are other methods of raising them, such as chopped fruits pressed together and placed on top, or a mixture of two parts of sugar to one of ground almonds, and flavour. A very general way is to take the Genoese waste cuttings, and mix with apricot purée, syrup, and a little red colour, flavour with rum, and pipe this mixture on top. In masking these, the dipping wire will have to be dispensed with, and they must be dipped with the aid of the fingers only. Care must be taken not to have the consistency of the fondant wrong, or the cake may show through and spoil the appearance. When all are dipped, pipe each one with the same coloured fondant as it is masked with, making a spiral from top to bottom, and finish by placing a small piece of crystallised flour or fruit on top, bearing in mind their colour and flavour, and decorating accordingly.

Q

SECTION IV., PLATE I.

BISCUITS—FLEUR D'ORANGE

10 Whites

$1\frac{1}{4}$ lbs. Sugar

7 ozs. Flour.

WHISK whites to a snow, add the sugar, and stir in the flour lightly with a wooden spoon. Lay out on greased and floured tins in fingers about $1\frac{1}{2}$ inches long. Dust over finely with icing sugar and bake.

TRESBURGS

THESE are made by cutting Madeira or any other plain cake into small cubes, and then cover them with the following mixture :—

3 Yolks

$\frac{1}{4}$ lb. Sugar

$\frac{1}{4}$ lb. Ground Almonds.

Completely cover with cobbled almonds, and bake to a nice brown colour.

FLEUR D'ORANGE.

TRESBURGS.

LANG DU CHAT.

QUEENS.

ALMOND SHAVINGS.

BUTTONS.

ALMOND RINGS.

BUTTER BISCUITS.

CHERRY BISCUIT.

COCOANUT DROPS.

FAIRY BISCUIT.

VANILLA FINGERS.

MOSS BISCUIT.

WINE BISCUITS.

𝔖ome 𝔑ovelties in 𝔅iscuits.

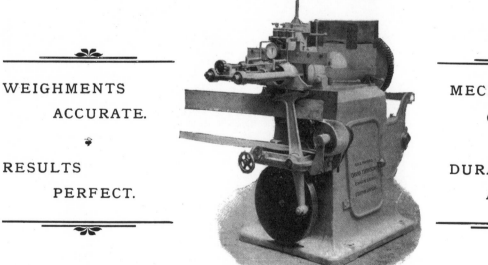

LANGUES DE CHAT

10 Whites

14 ozs. Icing Sugar

1 lb. Flour

$\frac{1}{2}$ pint of Cream.

WHISK up the whites, but not too stiff, add the sugar, and stir in the cream; add the flour, and, if too thick, add a little milk. Pipe out in thin and long fingers on greased and floured tins, and bake carefully. They should be white in the middle, with nicely browned edges. These can also be curled for shavings in the same way as the almond mixing given on next page.

QUEEN'S DROPS

14 ozs. Butter

10 ozs. Sugar

6 Eggs

14 ozs. Flour.

CREAM the butter and sugar, adding eggs gradually; stir in the flour; pipe out in small drops on paper and bake. Wash over with very thin water icing flavoured with lemon.

ALMOND SHAVINGS

18 ozs. Sugar

12 ozs. Ground Almonds

6 ozs. Flour

Whites.

MIX the sugar, almonds, and whites together, add the flour, and more whites till very thin. Colour half the mixture red. On a greased tin, dusted over with flour, pipe long thin fingers of white, and then one of red just touching the white. Bake lightly, and keep in the mouth of the oven whilst they are twisted into shape round a wooden spoon handle. These can also be laid out straight for Almond Langues de Chat similar to those given on previous page.

BUTTONS

1 lb. Butter

$1\frac{1}{4}$ lbs. Sugar

$1\frac{1}{2}$ lbs. Vienna Flour

$1\frac{1}{2}$ lbs. Eggs.

CREAM up the butter and sugar, add the eggs, and then the flour. Lay out small drops, or buttons, about the size of a shilling piece, with a Savoy tube on papered tins. Bake, and, when cold, stick them together in pairs with various flavoured and coloured fondant.

ALMOND OR COCOANUT RINGS

2 lbs. Flour

$1\frac{1}{2}$ lbs. Butter

1 lb. Sugar

$\frac{1}{2}$ lb. Ground Almonds

4 Eggs.

MAKE into paste in the ordinary way. Roll out barely $\frac{1}{4}$ inch thick, and cut out with a fluted cutter. Then, with a smaller cutter, punch out the centre. Egg over with whole egg, and dip the top of each into a mixture of equal parts of either cobbled almonds and small sugar nibs, or desiccated cocoanut and sugar nibs. Bake in a sound oven to a nice colour. These goods may be made either large enough to sell at $\frac{1}{2}$d. each or small enough to sell at 1s. per lb.

BUTTER BISCUITS

2 lbs. Fine Butter

2 lbs. Flour

1 lb. Sugar

4 Eggs

Essence of Vanilla.

MAKE the above into a good biscuit paste, in the usual way. Roll out thin and cut out with a fluted cutter. Bake in a sound oven, and dredge over with castor sugar, as the pans are taken from the oven.

CHERRY BISCUITS

3 lbs. Flour

$\frac{1}{4}$ lb. Ground Almonds

2 lbs. Butter

1 lb. Sugar

4 Eggs.

WORK the sugar, butter, almonds, and flour together and make into a paste with the eggs. When the dough is clear, roll out, not too thin, and cut out with a small round fluted cutter. Bring the edges of each together, as shown in the illustration, and press together firmly. Finish by putting a half cherry in each pocket end. Bake in a moderately sharp oven.

COCOANUT DROPS

1 lb. Sugar.

10 ozs. Cocoanut

Sufficient yolks of Eggs to form a stiff paste.

USE castor sugar and a medium desiccated cocoanut, mix to a stiff paste, just sufficiently moist to make the constituents stick together. Lay out with the fingers in small pyramids on wafer paper, and set to dry for half an hour. Bake in a quick oven, to a nice golden colour.

FAIRY BISCUITS

½ lb. Butter

½ lb. Castor Sugar

4 Eggs

½ lb. Flour

2 ozs. Currants

A Small Pinch of Powder.

CREAM up the butter and sugar in the usual way, giving it plenty of work. Beat in the eggs, and add the currants and flour. At this stage the mixture should not be beaten, or it may become tough. Lay out on slightly greased pan with a medium Savoy pipe, and bake in hot oven.

VANILLA FINGERS

2 lbs. Flour

$1\frac{1}{2}$ lbs. Butter

$1\frac{1}{2}$ lbs. Sugar

4 Eggs

Essence of Vanilla.

MAKE a clear biscuit paste of the above, in the usual way. Roll out in a sheet about $\frac{3}{8}$ of an inch thick. Divide in two with a knife, egg over each portion, and cover evenly with dry castor sugar, one portion white and the other pink. Then cut out in small fingers about $2\frac{1}{2}$ inches long by $\frac{1}{2}$ an inch wide. Place on clean baking-sheets, just close enough not to touch, and bake.

MOSS BISCUITS

2 lbs. Flour

$1\frac{1}{4}$ lbs. Butter

$\frac{3}{4}$ lb. Sugar

3 Eggs.

MAKE this into a smooth paste in the usual way by mixing it all up together and working down under hand. To give the biscuits the necessary mossy appearance, the paste may either be rubbed with a wooden spoon through a medium wire sieve, but a better, although a home-made method, is to co-opt the potato-masher from the kitchen and force the mixing through this. Take up the paste so treated in small irregular bits and place on a baking-sheet. Allow them to stand for an hour or so to set, and then bake off in a sharp oven.

WINE BISCUITS

THE name of Wine Biscuit is applicable to a large variety of shapes and flavours. The following mixing may be

R

THE BOOK OF CAKES

130

used for what may be called the ground work of this class :—

4 lbs. Flour

2 lbs. Butter

2 lbs. Sugar

8 Eggs.

Squeeze the butter down well, and rub it into the flour. Make a bay and put in the sugar and eggs, which must then be thoroughly stirred to mix. Work the whole mixing down under hand until it is clear and fine.

The dough thus made may be broken into any number of pieces, to each of which a distinctive flavour and appearance can be given by the addition of caraway seeds, small currants, ground almonds, desiccated cocoanut, etc. Roll out each kind separately, and, when thin enough, cut out with a different shaped cutter to each variety. Thus plain may be cut round; caraway, crescent; currants, square; cocoanut, heart shaped; almonds, pear shaped; etc. Further variety may be given by washing the top of the rolled-out dough, before cutting out, and then sprinkling with desiccated cocoanut, cherries (chopped and dried), cobbled almonds, etc.

SECTION IV., PLATE II.

ALMOND GOODS—Nos. 1 and 2.
DUTCH MACAROONS

3 lbs. Castor Sugar

2 lbs. Ground Almonds

About 18 Whites.

MIX all thoroughly well together in a bowl—enough whites being added that when laid out the macaroons just run smooth on top.

Colour half the mixing red, and lay out on papered tins in slightly oblong drops of a suitable size; place them in a drying cupboard or prover till dry enough; they will take about five hours in an ordinary side prover. Then draw a pin through the centre of the crust of each one and bake in a cool oven. They will crack and throw up in the centre. When baked, wash the backs of the paper with hot water; they will then come off easily; stick them together in pairs, and they are finished.

In illustration No. 1 they are shown in a different form, being laid out in long fingers, which makes a pleasing variety from the orthodox shape.

No. 3. ALMOND APRICOTINES

THESE can also be made with ground Barcelonas taken in the same proportion as the almonds.

2 lbs. Sugar

1½ lbs. Ground Almonds

Whites.

Mix the sugar and almonds with enough whites of egg to make it of an ordinary macaroon consistency, and beat up. Lay out on stiff paper in drops; cover the tops with ground Barcelona kernels, or, failing this, use cocoanut, and bake. When cold, stick together with apricot puree.

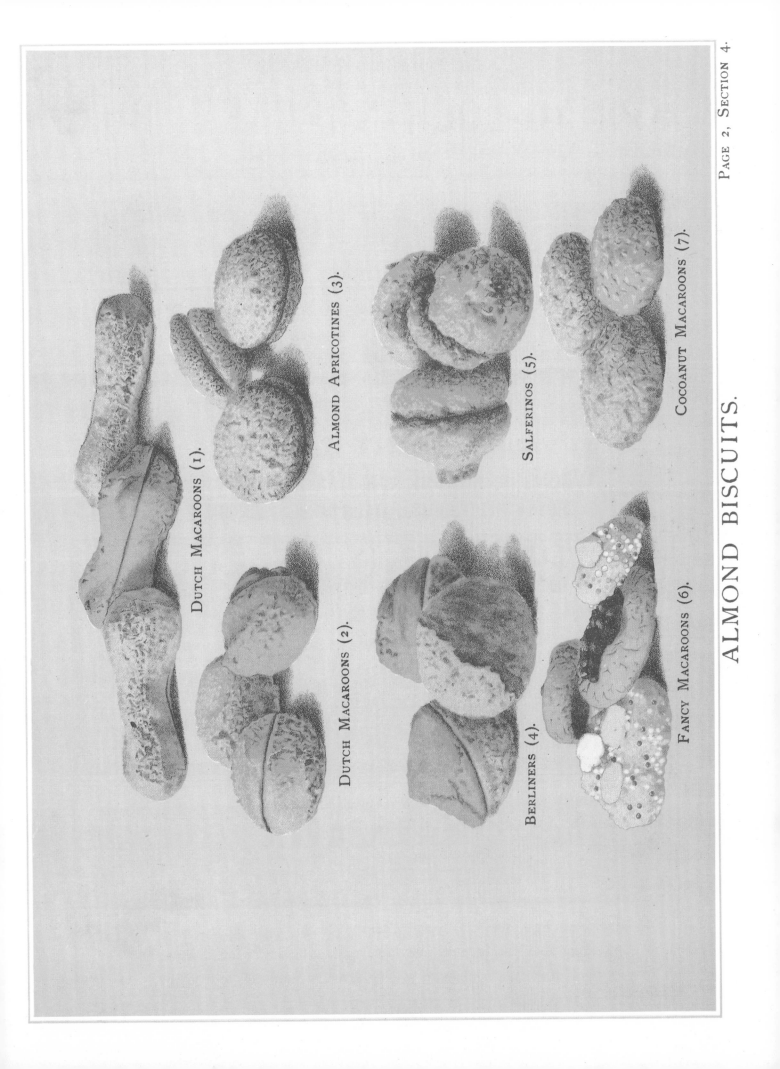

Dutch Macaroons (1).

Almond Apricotines (3).

Dutch Macaroons (2).

Salferinos (5).

Berliners (4).

Cocoanut Macaroons (7).

Fancy Macaroons (6).

ALMOND BISCUITS.

No. 4. BERLINERS

1½ lbs. Sugar

1 lb. Almonds

8 or 9 Whites.

MIX all thoroughly together; lay out on papered tins, in drops about the size of half a crown, and dry in the prover for from four to six hours. Draw a pin across the centre and bake. Stick them together in pairs with apricot preserve.

No. 5. SOLFERINOS

1 lb. Sugar

6 ozs. Ground Almonds

2 ozs. Cocoanut

Whites.

KNOCK up the mixing as for macaroons, and pipe out on stiff paper rather larger than a shilling piece. Sprinkle coarse cocoanut over, and place together in pairs with raspberry preserve between.

No. 6. FANCY MACAROONS

$\frac{3}{4}$ lb. Sugar

$\frac{1}{2}$ lb. Ground Almonds

Whites.

BEAT up the sugar and almonds with enough whites to form macaroon consistency, and lay out in various fancy shapes on wafer paper. Sprinkle nonpareils over the majority, and decorate the remainder with cherries, angelica, etc. When half-baked, press the finger down in the middle of those covered with the nonpareils, and, when baked and cold, fill the indentations so made with various coloured fondant.

No. 7. COCOANUT MACAROONS

1 lb. Sugar

4 ozs. Almonds

4 ozs. Cocoanut

Whites.

MIX all thoroughly together, beat up well at macaroon consistency, lay out in drops the size of a two-shilling piece on wafer-papered tins, sprinkle desiccated cocoanut over, and bake.

SECTION IV., PLATES III. AND IV.

PETITS FOURS SEC

THESE are also known under the names of Rout Biscuits, Parisian Routs, etc. They are made in most first-class shops, and, owing to their pretty appearance and fine eating qualities, they are great favourites at afternoon teas and parties.

They are by no means difficult to make, though care is required throughout in their manufacture, and especially so in the baking. Neatness in laying out, decorating and displaying is essential if one wishes to make a really good show.

They should be made from sugar and ground almonds, though a very respectable article can be turned out by using the marzipan paste sold by various firms. In the latter event the same quantity of paste should be taken as ground almonds here given—

1 lb. Castor Sugar

1 lb. Ground Almonds

About 5 or 6 Whites, according to size.

Mix the whole thoroughly together into a rather tight mixture—not nearly so soft as for macaroons, but do not beat it up. A very good plan is to now place the bowl containing the mixing on the gas-stove or fire and warm it through. This partly cooks and softens it, making it considerably easier to form quickly into the shapes. Place some of the mixing in a bag with a star pipe affixed. Some prefer a rather large, deep cut, star tube, others a smaller and finely cut one; in the latter case, they require to be gone over twice, making a top and bottom to each. The last is perhaps the neatest, the first is easier and quicker. Lay out on greased tins, which have been dusted with flour, the various fancy shapes shown in the illustrations. Decorate them with cherries, angelica, silver dragees and fruit, and allow them to stand and dry until the following day, when they should be baked on double tins in a hot oven and nicely browned, and then washed over with simple syrup or a solution of gum arabic and water. Place neatly in rows on a tray, and they are ready for the shop.

PETITS FOURS SEC.

PETITS FOURS SEC.

SECTION V., PLATES I., II., AND III.

SPECIMENS OF PIPING

IN this section are shown some very good examples of commercial piping, including Piped Flowers, Scrolls, Lettering and Monograms.

PIPED FLOWERS

It is exceedingly difficult to explain in print how to pipe even the most simple of flowers, and it is as difficult for the reader to follow and understand the instructions.

PRIMROSES

On plate 1 are shown some Primroses, and as these are perhaps as simple as any, we will start with them. The tools required are a few small-sized flower nails or moulds and a small leaf tube. (See illustrations, p. 143.) Have the icing beaten up well, so that it will stand when on the nail, colour it pale yellow and place in the paper cornet in which the tube has already been fixed. The nails should be slightly greased or the flower will stick when dry. Hold the nail in the left hand, rest the thick end of the tube on the head of the nail and form the first petal with a slight pressure of the thumb on the cornet. Do six petals in all and pipe the centres with deep yellow icing.

NARCISSUS

Two rows of Narcissi of various sizes—one white and the second pale yellow—are shown on the same sheet. At the bottom of plate 2 the different stages in the manufacture of a Pheasant-eyed Narcissus is shown. For these the icing must be very well up and rather tighter than for ordinary work. For the white variety have just a little blue in the icing and let the yellow be pale. Hold the nail and tube as for the primrose, but in this instance, make the petal longer and larger, causing the last part of the leaf shown to stand well up; have the commencement of each petal under the one pre-ceding and over the one following, start the second well under the first and so on until the six have been formed.

Then with a fine pipe of deep yellow icing form the centre cup, starting small at the bottom and getting larger towards the top; then go over it with a fine pipe of deep red.

A very pretty effect can be obtained by the judicious use of these flowers.

Violets

The small blue flowers shown are called Violets in the illustration, but this is a libel on a pretty and popular flower. They are quite easy to pipe and can be done on nails or on a flat piece of tin or glass which must be slightly greased. Run a fine streak of dark blue icing down the side of a cornet fitted with a small leaf tube and fill with pale blue; pipe one petal on the prepared surface and then pipe the deep yellow centre with a plain tube, then add two or three more leaves on top.

Forget-me-nots

Tubes are made and sold for piping these, but they have the great drawback of making all the flowers of exactly the same size, whereas, when piping a spray of Forget-me-nots, they should gradually get smaller towards the end of the spray. The best method is to use a plain paper cornet, cut the point to the required size and pipe each petal separately. Use a light and dark blue in the same pipe and fill in the centres in deep yellow.

Rosebuds

Pipe the centre with a plain tube, in a deep shade of whatever colour your Roses are. Then pipe the fine lines in green over them, adding the stem and bulb.

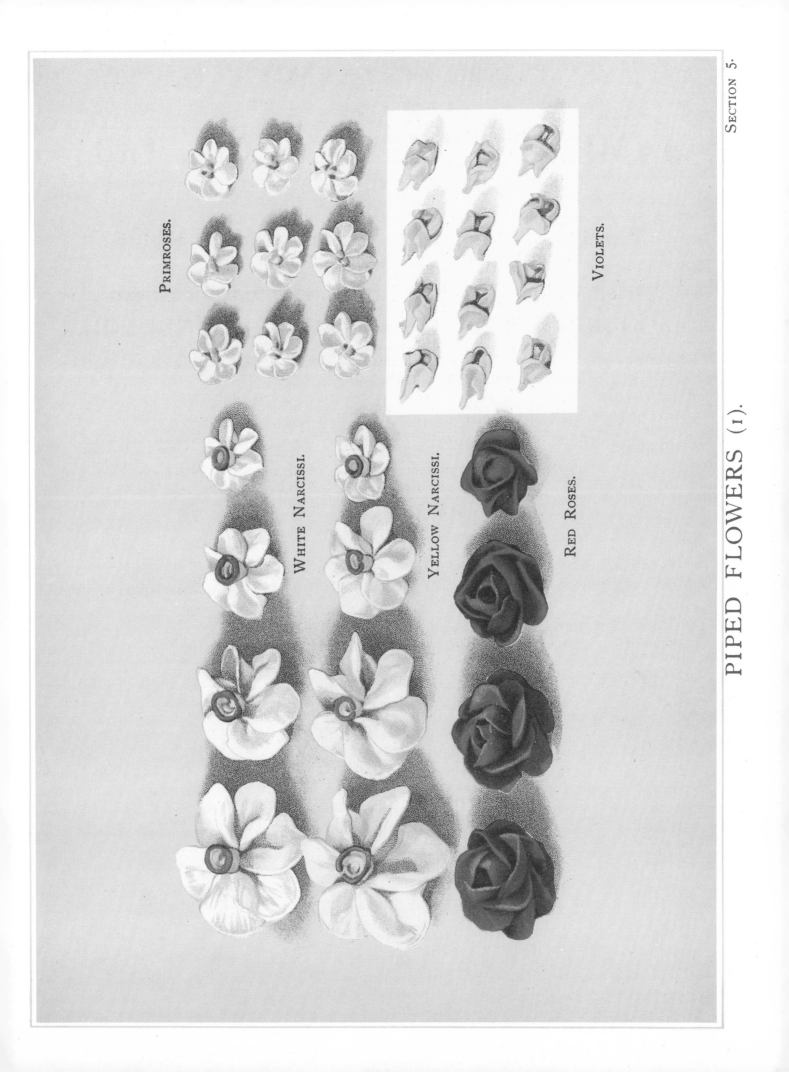

PRIMROSES.

VIOLETS.

WHITE NARCISSI.

YELLOW NARCISSI.

RED ROSES.

PIPED FLOWERS (1).

ESTABLISHED 1859.

JAMES FLEMING & CO., Ltd.,

SUGAR, SPICE AND RICE MILLERS.

MANUFACTURERS OF

Marzipan, Almond Paste and Fondant Icings.

IMPORTERS OF

Dried Fruits, Cherries, Almonds, Essences, &c.

19 ALBERT STREET (Leith Walk), EDINBURGH.

SUGARS.

All kinds of Sugars for Confectioners' Uses, including :—

SIFTED SUGARS.
GROUND SUGARS.
SIFTED CASTOR.
BUN NIBS.

ICING SUGAR—
Finest Prepared.
Piping No. I.
,, ,, II.
,, ,, III.
Confectioners'.

FINEST FONDANT ICINGS—
White.
Pink.
Heliotrope.
Chocolate.
Lemon.

FONDANT ICINGS—*Contd.*
Yellow.
(In 28 lb. tins and $\frac{1}{2}$ and 1 cwt. drums, flavoured with Vanilla, Lemon, Orange, Rose, &c., and with fresh fruits in their season.)

MARZIPAN PLATES, SHORTBREAD AND CAKE ORNAMENTS.
MARZIPAN AND ALMOND PASTES—Finest Qualities.

DRIED FRUITS.

CURRANTS—
Vostizza, Finest.
Panariti.
Patras.
Zante.
Amalias.
Pyrgos.
Provincial.

SULTANAS—
Greeks.
Carabourna.
Vourla.
Smyrna.
RAISINS—
Valencia, Seedless.
Muscatels, Seedless.

PEELS—
Drained and Candied.
Citron.
Orange in boxes and kegs.
Lemon.
GINGER, PRESERVED—
Chips, Drained and Candied.
Cubes

ALMONDS.

ALMONDS—
Jordan, Fine.
,, Good.
,, Blanched.
Alicante, Finest.
,, Fine.
Valencia, Finest.

ALMONDS—*Contd.*
Valencia, Fine.
Malaga, Flat.
Catania, Flat.
French Bitter, Finest.
Ground, in cwt. cases, 28 lb. boxes, $\frac{1}{2}$ and 1 lb. tins neatly labelled.

ALMONDS—*Contd.*
Nibs, 3 sizes.
Flake.
Split.
Stripes.
Blanched.
Paste.

HAZEL NUTS.
WALNUTS.
PINONES.
PISTACHIO KERNELS.
COCOANUT.

SPICES.

CINNAMON.
GINGER.
CASSIA.

CASSIA BUDS.
CLOVES.
CARRAWAYS.

CORIANDER.
FINEST MIXED SPICES.
PIMENTO.

MACE.
NUTMEGS.
&c.

ESSENCES.

CASSIA.
CHERRY.
CINNAMON.
CLOVES.
LEMON—
Finest.
II.

GINGER.
ORANGE—
Bitter.
Sweet.
ORANGE FLOWER WATER.
PEAR.

PEPPERMINT.
PINEAPPLE.
RASPBERRY.
RASPBERRY FRUIT.
RATAFIA.
ROSE.

ROSE WATER.
STRAWBERRY.
,, Cream Flavour.
VANILLA.
VANILLINE CRYSTALS.
LEMON CURD.

CAKE COLOURS.

CHERRY RED, APPLE GREEN, LEMON, YELLOW and COCHINEAL.

GLACE FRUITS.

ASSORTED FRUITS.
APRICOTS.

ANGELICA.
CHERRIES.

CHINOIS.
PINEAPPLE.

TARTAR—
Finest B.P., Test 98 %.
Commercial, 92 and 95 %.

VOLATILE.
CHOCOLATE POWDER.

CHOCOLATE BLOCK.
GELATINE.

Lilies of the Valley

First pipe the stems with the droops in a dark shade of green, then pipe the leaves in a paler green and add the Lilies to the stems, using a medium-sized plain pipe.

Maidenhair Fern

Use a small cornet containing brown icing, cut the point fine and pipe the stems of the spray. Next, with a tube of the same size, filled with the proper shades of green, add the leaves. Some little practice will be required before this can be done easily and quickly.

Shamrock

Use the same shades of green for this—pale and dark. Pipe the stems first, adding the leaves with a slightly larger tube.

Pansies and Violas

For these use a medium-sized leaf tube; put in a streak of dark blue, and fill up the cornet with pale blue icing.

Rest the thick end on the nail and form the three petals on one side of the flower, add the two yellow ones in the same way on the other side. Violas, a cross between a Pansy and a Violet, are made in somewhat the same way, but the petals are a trifle longer and narrower, whereas in the Pansy they should be wide. Pipe the centres with deep yellow.

ROSES

Remarks on the formation of roses apply to all the varieties shown, the colouring only being different. Two basins of icing should be prepared of the colour required, one containing dark and the other a paler shade of icing, the former for the centres, and the latter for the outer petals. Have the icing stiffer than for ordinary work. On plate 2 a rose is shown in the various stages. First pipe a fair-sized dot in the centre of the nail, then with a medium-sized rose or leaf tube, pipe a band round it in the darkest shade (*a*), against these pipe three fair-sized petals leaning over and almost hiding the band (*b*). When all have been done in this manner, take the paler shade, and with another tube of the same size, pipe the two outer rows of leaves (*c*) and (*d*).

The smaller half-opened roses are piped in a different way. The centres are first piped in the deeper shade as for the large ones and then dried. A cornet containing the paler shade is then used, with a medium-sized rose tube affixed. First pipe a petal on the

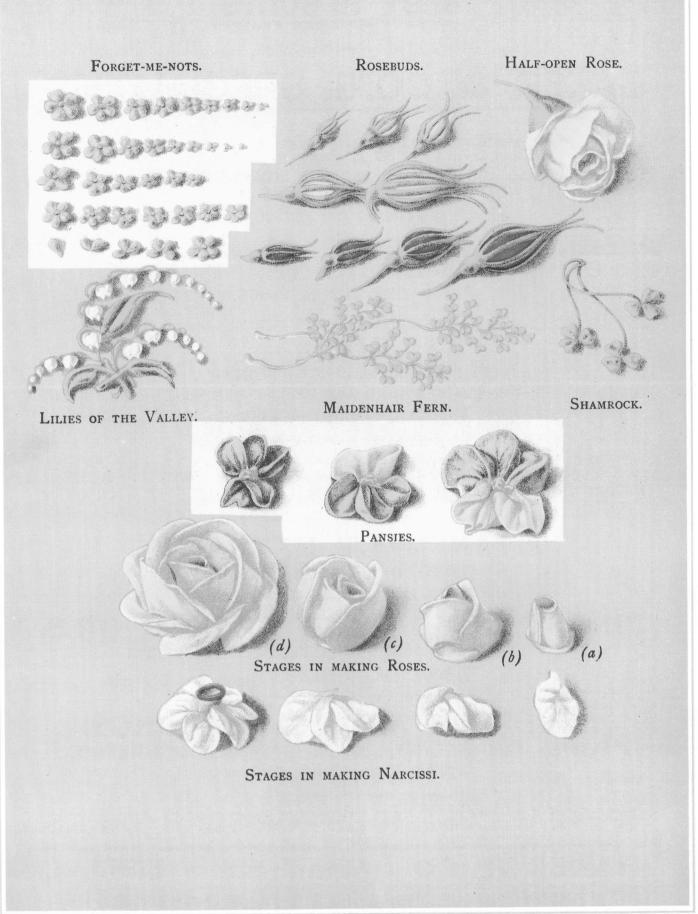

FORGET-ME-NOTS.

ROSEBUDS.

HALF-OPEN ROSE.

LILIES OF THE VALLEY.

MAIDENHAIR FERN.

SHAMROCK.

PANSIES.

(d)   *(c)*   *(b)*   *(a)*

STAGES IN MAKING ROSES.

STAGES IN MAKING NARCISSI.

PIPED FLOWERS (2).

prepared nail or sheet of tin, and place the dried centre on, then continue piping the remainder of the leaves, covering the base of the centre and making it look as natural as possible.

The deep red roses shown are coloured after being piped, by dusting over with powdered carmine.

A good way to do this is to use a soft tooth-brush by dipping it in the powder and drawing the finger across the bristles when the powder will fly on to the object to be coloured.

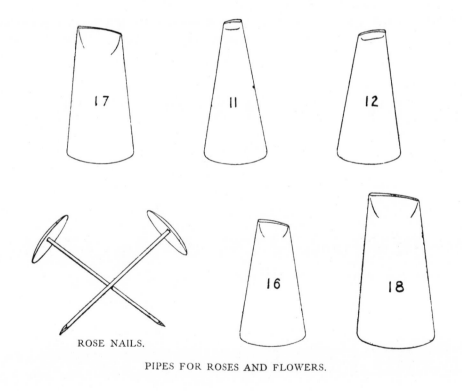

ROSE NAILS.

PIPES FOR ROSES AND FLOWERS.

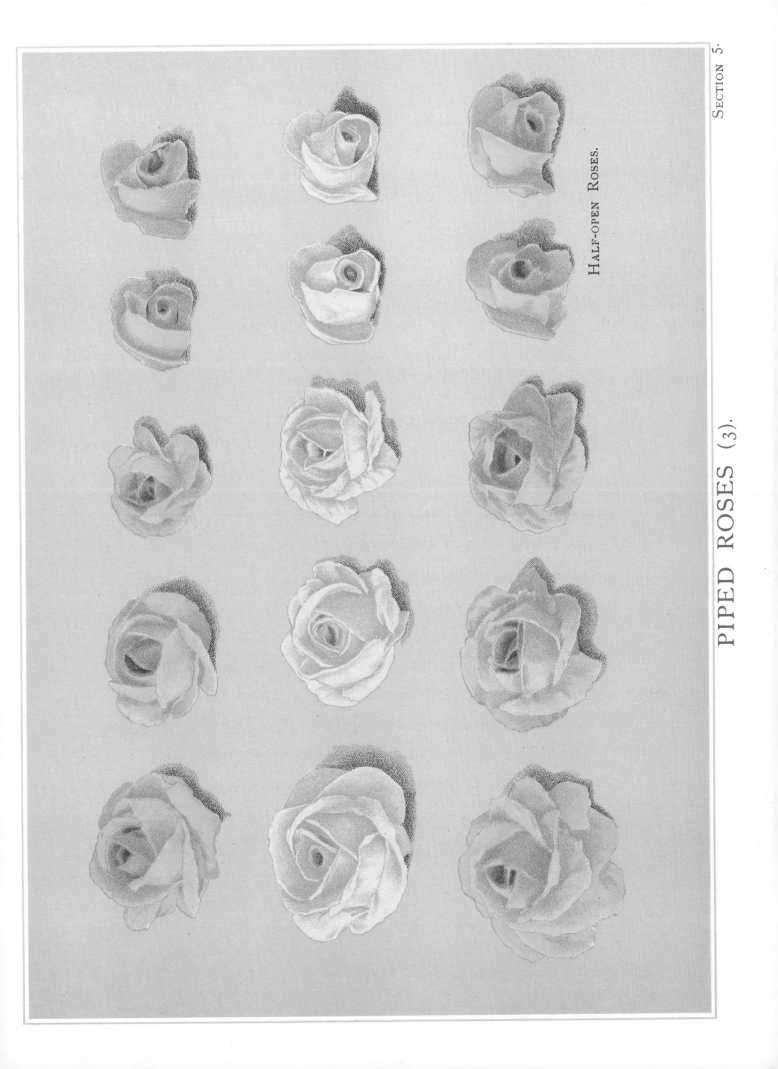

HALF-OPEN ROSES.

PIPED ROSES (3).

SECTION V., PLATE IV.

THE PIPING OF SCROLLS

TWO specimens of scrolls are shown on plate 4 of Section V. The first is piped in pink on a pale pink ground. The main part of the scroll is an alternating or reversing curve, and it is necessary, in order to ensure that the scroll be quite true and correct, that these must first be got quite exact, and then the attendant curves, scrolls, and lines are added on in their proper places   Use a plain tube pipe throughout.

The second example is done in white on a white ground, and in the original had the appearance of being carved. The scroll is first outlined, and then each line carefully built up, one on the other, some three or four times.

It is unnecessary to state that this requires some amount of patience, and we would hardly recommend this example for ordinary work on the side of a cake, although the first is quite suitable and commercial.

SECTION V., PLATE V.

LETTERING AND WRITING

SIX examples are shown, four of which were piped in **a** few minutes, and are given as specimens of ordinary writing such as may be used on a shilling gateau or a decorated cake.   For articles of this description the writing must be done very quickly and neatly, because laboured work does not look well on such goods and saving of time is a great object when a large number has to be decorated.   The first example on plate 5, example 1, " A Merry Christmas," is piped in ordinary script, though the letters are rather elongated; the upstrokes are thin and down strokes thick in the centre.   The colours used are two shades of pink in the same pipe.

The next example is the word " Chocolate " as used on Chocolate gateaux.   The letters are formed after the style of Old English and can be done very quickly.   The colours are the same as in the first.

T

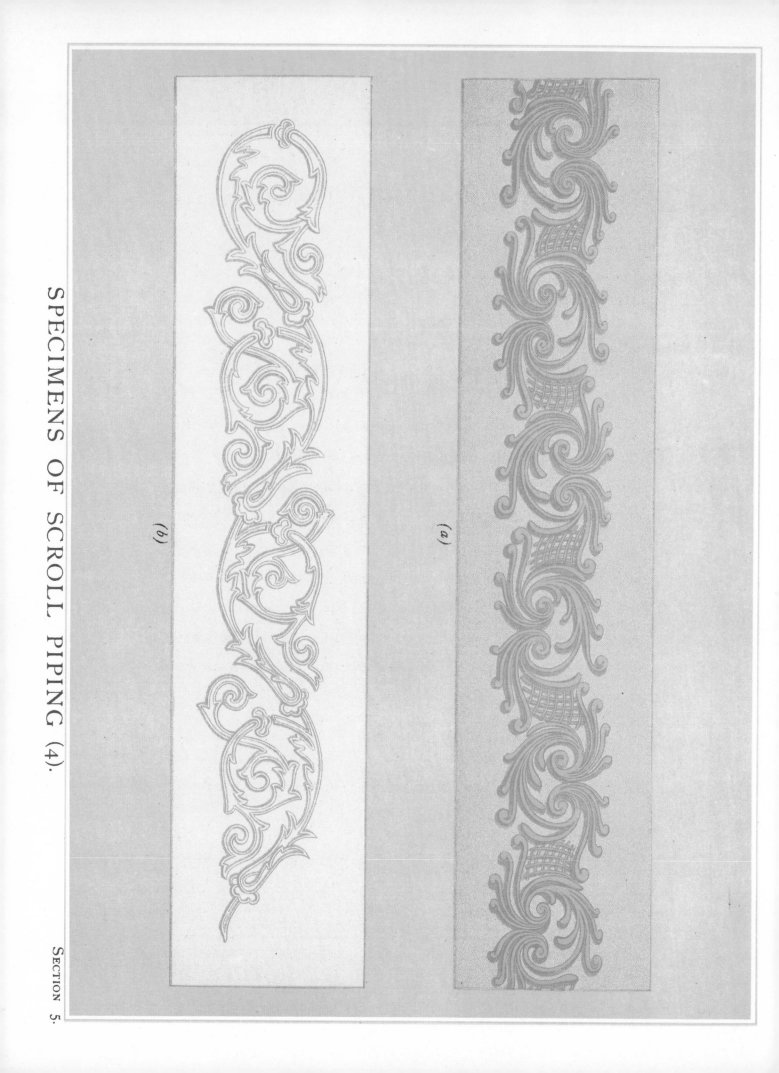

SPECIMENS OF SCROLL PIPING (4).

(b)

(a)

(1)

A Merry Christmas

(2)

Chocolate

(3)

New Year Greetings

EXAMPLES OF LETTERING AND WRITING (5).

The third, " New Year Greetings," is in the same style of letter as the first.　The letters are first piped in yellow and then the lower parts gone over with heliotrope as shown in the illustration.

The first and second examples on the next sheet, plate 6, were amongst the first prize lot in the Piped Specimen class some years ago. "A Merry Christmas" (1) is piped in round hand.　The ivory colour is made by using pale yellow and a streak of brown in the same pipe.

The " Many Happy Returns " (2) is done in Old English characters which look very well indeed on medallions or decorated cakes, etc.　The great point to observe is to have the letters perfectly even and well-spaced, as good writing is often spoiled by uneven spacing.　This example was first piped in pale pink and afterwards outlined with a deeper shade of the same colour.

The last example shown is for a Strawberry gateau (3) and is a style of letter that looks effective and yet is very quickly done. The upstroke is thin and plain, but on coming down, the pipe is given a peculiar jumping movement to form the rope-like down stroke; it can be either gone over with a fine line or left.　The colours are two shades of pink in the same tube.

(1) A Merry Christmas

(2) Many Happy Returns

(3) Strawberry

EXAMPLES OF LETTERING AND WRITING (6).

MONOGRAMS

FIVE examples of monograms are given. We give three examples of two-letter monograms and two of three letters, which make a fine collection. To our minds monogram piping is a most interesting study and will well repay the student's careful attention. Great care with neatness and accuracy is of course required, but apart from this no special skill in the art of piping is called into play.

It is always the best plan to work from a copy—first work out the letters you require to form into a monogram on paper, then copy from the design thus obtained.

On plate 8 are shown two rather more complicated examples of two-letter monograms. The first—No. 7, S T—is piped in pale pink and yellow, these are simply outlined and not filled in. The lines are built up one on the other, carefully and neatly, and the dots, etc., piped in a darker shade.

MONOGRAM PIPING (8).   Section 5.

The second, No. 8, on the same sheet, consists of the letters E S and is piped in pale green and brown. The same remarks apply to this as to the last. It is perhaps a trifle more difficult to execute owing to the scroll added to the S which does not appear in the others.

We now come to a very pretty three-letter monogram J E G (illustration 9) in pale shades of yellow, pink and green respectively. Each letter having more ornament attached and being disjointed, will, if piped straight off, be found difficult to get balanced correctly. The remarks on the two-letter combinations apply equally here. Outline the three letters first before attempting to build them up. Use a good plain pipe and have the icing in good condition.

The next, No. 10, is the best monogram of the series. The illustration M D speaks for itself. The three letters G E M are piped in delicate shades of pink, yellow and green, outlined and filled in, built up, and the attendant dots, lines, and scrolls put in position in the manner already described.

MONOGRAM PIPING (9).

It Pays to use the Best

W. & M. Pumphrey, Ltd
Sugar Millers
THORNABY · ON · TEES, LONDON & GLASGOW

MONOGRAM PIPING (10).

MONOGRAM PIPING (11).

At the Sign of the Sugar Loaves

TRADE MARK

BRIDAL Icing SUGAR

REG. 1896

W. & M. Pumphrey, Ltd

Sugar Millers

THORNABY-ON-TEES, LONDON & GLASGOW

TRADE MARK

BANQUET Caster SUGAR

REG. 1884

A K, on plate 11, is a plain but striking example, the A being in heliotrope and the K in pale yellow. This makes a pretty combination and adds to the beauty of the whole. Outline the letters in their respective colours and fill in between with the same coloured icing made a little slacker. Allow this to dry and then build up the outlines and fill in the dots with darker shades of self-colours.

As we have already stated, no extraordinary amount of skill is required for monogram piping, but plenty of patience, care and exactness is indispensable.

SECTION VI., ILLUSTRATIONS I., II., III.

SHORTBREAD

ILLUSTRATIONS are given of three cakes of shortbread. No. 1 is quite plain, No. 2 is decorated with preserved fruit, and No. 3 is iced and piped. This ever popular cake is too little understood by English confectioners, with the result that very little good shortbread is ever seen that has been made south of the Tweed. The recipe given below, if carefully worked, will give the finest results.

17 lbs. Soft Home Milled Flour

3 lbs. American Patent Flour

2 lbs. Self-Raising or Patent Flour

2 lbs. Ground Rice

6 lbs. Castor Sugar

5 lbs. Fresh Butter

8 lbs. Salt Butter

8 Large Eggs.

Sift half of the sugar through the flour and ground rice, and then proceed to break the whole of the butter in. Make a bay,

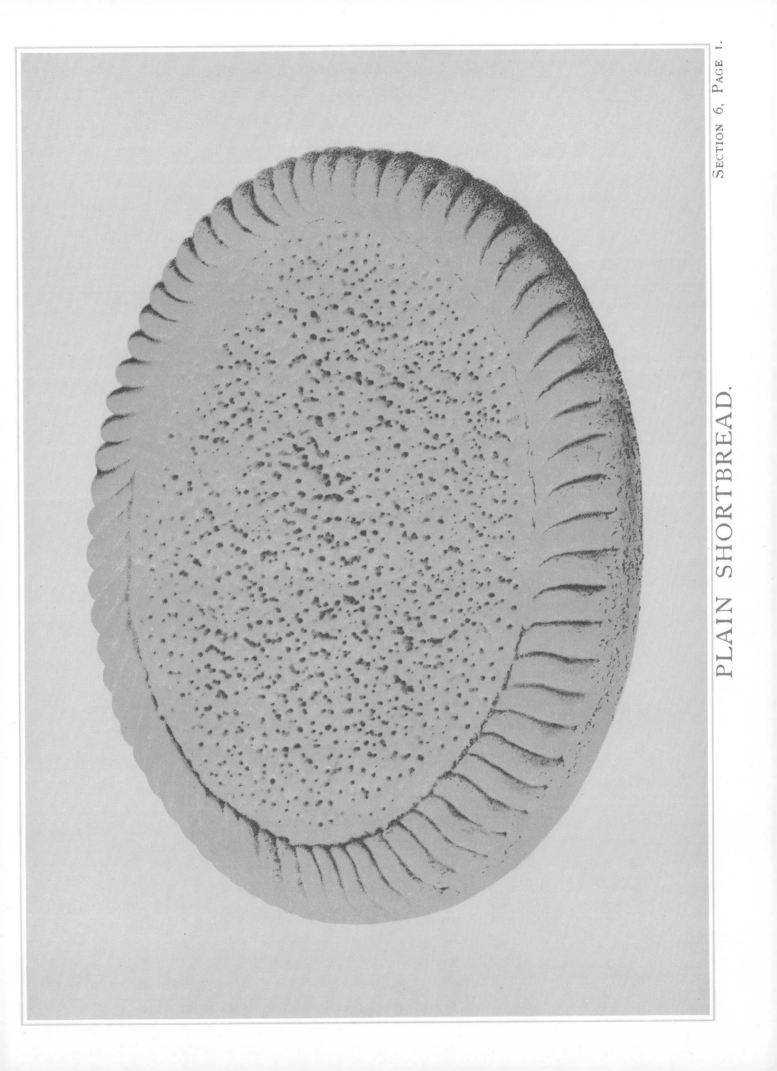

PLAIN SHORTBREAD.

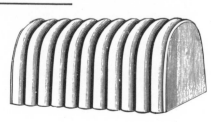

put in it the remainder of the sugar and the eggs, and carefully rub the whole down smooth. The dough is then ready for use.

In making shortbread it is very necessary that special care should be taken with all the ingredients. In the recipe the flour is divided into three parts—and this is practically essential. The patent or self-raising flour is made by carefully sifting over two or three times the following mixture:—

> 21 lbs. Flour
>
> 7 ozs. Cream of Tartar
>
> 4 ozs. Carbonate of Soda.

This should be kept stored in a dry tub ready for use. Divide the paste into suitably-sized pieces, mould up round, roll out flat about 1 inch thick, and docker all over. The edges may either be crimped or pinched, or the whole cake may be blocked out in wooden blocks which are sold for the purpose. To bake, place the cakes of shortbread on a baking-sheet, either with or without a block-tin ring round each, and bake in a medium to cool oven.

To decorate with fruit (No. 2). Dip some fine coloured preserved fruits (crystallised or glacé) in hot water to take off the sugar. Cut up into fancy shapes and attach to the cake in any design required, with a little icing. Finish by taking a fine cornet of icing and piping the remainder of the design.

To decorate with icing (No. 3). This needs no directions, as the details are all clearly set out in the illustration. First run a circle of icing round inside the crimping, and, when dry, carefully pipe, using a little angelica to give a relief to the pink and white.

SHORTBREAD VARIETIES

The following few recipes (although not illustrated) will be found useful, and are thoroughly commercial.

THIN SHORTBREAD

1 lb. 2 ozs. Flour

$\frac{1}{2}$ lb. Butter

10 ozs. Sugar

3 Eggs.

Make into a stiff paste and work down smooth under hand. Roll out the whole evenly on a slab to a thickness of about $\frac{3}{16}$ of an inch, docker finely all over, cut out with a sharp knife into oblong pieces about 3 inches by $1\frac{1}{4}$ inches, or larger if required. Place on a baking-sheet and bake.

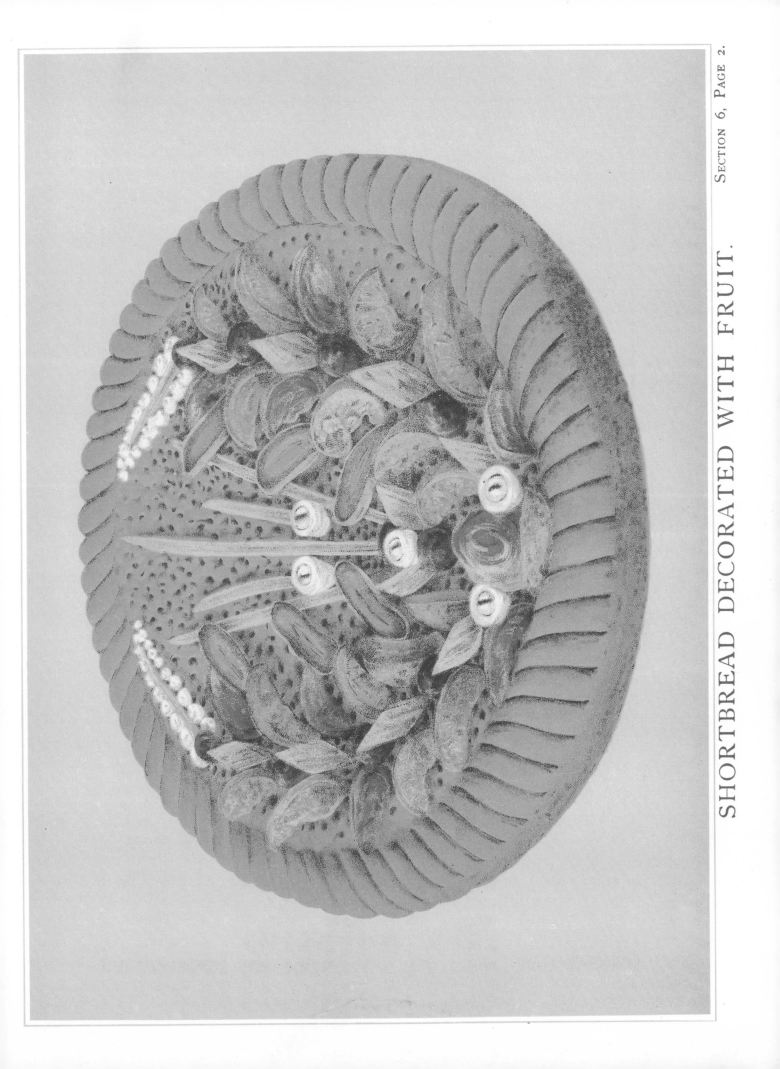

SHORTBREAD DECORATED WITH FRUIT.

SECTION 6, PAGE 2.

"The meeting sweet that made me thrill. The sweetmeat almost sweeter still."—MELLO-MALLO.

SIMPLICITY itself to use, Mello-Mallo is the filling which really fills—never falls away, hardens or changes colour, and because no fat is used in its manufacture, can never go sour or rancid. Beaten up with egg-whites its bulk increases to eight times its size. Although a dainty, billowy cream, it possesses sufficient "body" for chocolate or fondant dipping.

Mello-Mallo is an economy to use, as, apart from its low cost, we undertake to give expert technical advice on how to use it for all kinds of new and "trade-increasing" fancies. Let us have your order for a trial cwt. *now*, and remember one cwt. of Mello-Mallo goes as far as many cwt. of butter cream.

No Preservative of any kind in Mello-Mallo

Scottish Agents—
HUGH BAIRD & SONS, LTD.
29 St. Vincent Place, Glasgow

Sole Manufacturers—
A. BELLAMY & CO., LTD., 23 Harp Lane
LONDON, E.C. 3

Factory : WOLVERHAMPTON
and at CARDIFF

Mello-Mallo
THE DAINTY CREAM

TWO-PENNY SHORTBREAD

5 lbs. Flour

$2\frac{1}{2}$ lbs. Butter

$1\frac{1}{4}$ lbs. Sugar

4 Eggs.

Moisten with a drop of Milk.

Mix the ingredients into a paste and work down smooth under hand. Weigh off into pieces $\frac{3}{4}$ lb. each and mould up round. Roll out each piece to the thickness of about $\frac{1}{2}$ inch and pinch round the border. Docker the top all over. Then with a sharp knife divide it into four, in the same way as scones are cut, and place close together, with cut edges just touching, on baking-sheets and bake. When the shortbread comes from the oven, dredge lightly all over with castor sugar.

PENNY SHORTBREADS

10 lbs. Flour

4 lbs. Butter

4 lbs. Sugar

24 Eggs

Essence of Lemon.

U

Rub the butter into the flour. Make a bay, and put into it the sugar, eggs, and essence. Thoroughly work up and make smooth under hand. The paste may be shaped either by blocking in a spindle-shaped wooden block, or by being rolled out thin on a slab, and then cut out with a spindle-shaped cutter and pinched. The latter is probably the quicker, but the former more reliable as to regularity, as in this case the mixture may be weighed off, 7 ozs. being divided into four. Place on baking-sheets, put a small bit of citron in the middle of each, and bake.

In some districts these goods are known as Waterloos, but why shortbreads should be called so it is not easy to guess.

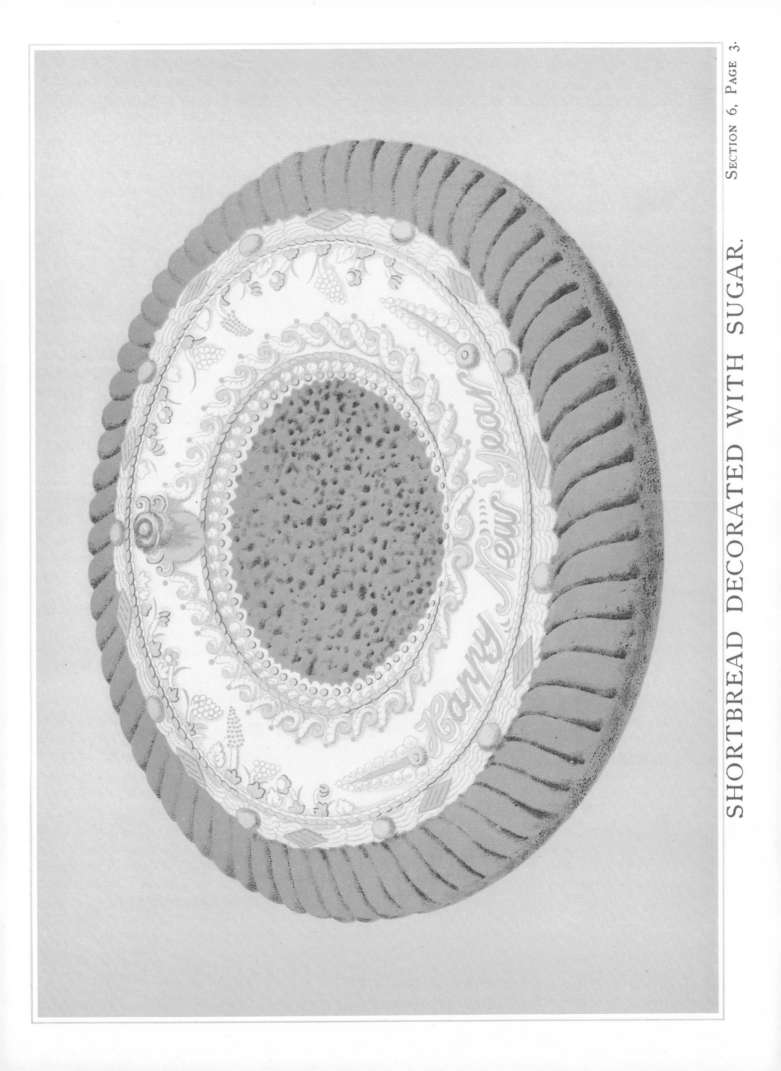

SHORTBREAD DECORATED WITH SUGAR.

The Leading Manufacturer.

Bakery Fittings, all sizes in stock.

Marble-top Tables a speciality.

Confectioners' Cabinets made in various designs.

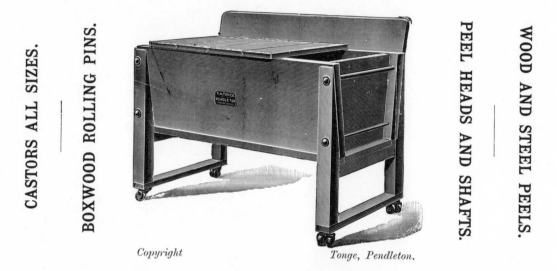

CASTORS ALL SIZES.

BOXWOOD ROLLING PINS.

PEEL HEADS AND SHAFTS.

WOOD AND STEEL PEELS.

Copyright

Tonge, Pendleton.

Your enquiries shall have my prompt attention.

ILLUSTRATED CATALOGUES POST FREE.

Telegrams: "Tonge, Irlam's-o'-th'-Height."

2 words.

Telephone No. 101 Pendleton.

T. H. TONGE,

The Bakery Fitter,

PENDLETON.

SECTION VII., PLATE I.

TWO SAVOY MOULDS

THE main difficulties to be surmounted in turning out good Savoy moulds appear to be in the preparation of the mould and in the baking. The greatest care must be observed in both these operations or the result may be a most unsightly production. Prepare the moulds by rubbing out with a clean cloth, taking care that all crevices are well cleaned out, and grease with some creamed lard, dust out with flour and sugar, and stand them upright in a round cake or bread tin. Put some paper round to support and protect the bottom from the heat, and tie a wide band of paper round the base of the mould.

$2\frac{1}{2}$ lbs. Eggs

2 lbs. 6 ozs. Sugar

$2\frac{1}{4}$ lbs. Flour.

Place the eggs and sugar in the machine or bowl and knock up well, then stir in the flour lightly, and fill the moulds less than three parts full and bake in not too warm an oven. If they should appear to be colouring too much, cover with a sheet of paper to protect them.

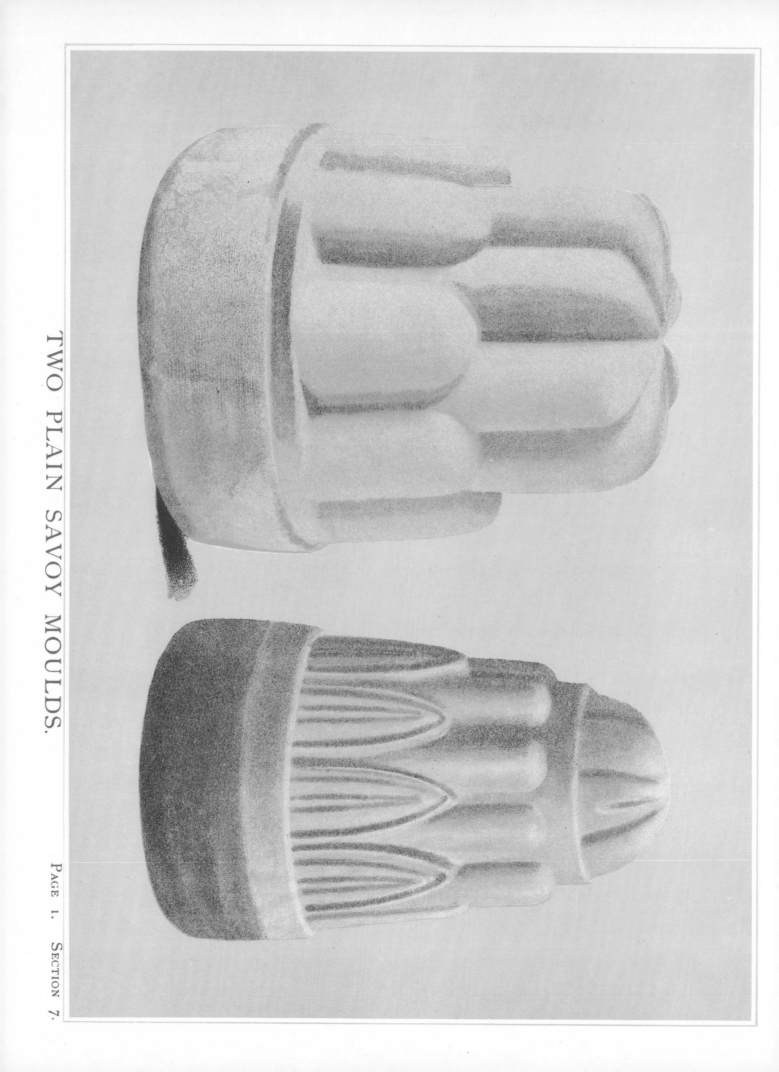

TWO DECORATED SAVOY MOULDS.

SECTION VII., PLATE II.

DECORATED SAVOY MOULDS

THE first of those shown is iced in two colours—the base, as far as the points of the Gothic window-like portions, is a pretty shade of heliotrope, whilst the remainder is a pale primrose yellow. The lines on the pillars are built up one on the other to a considerable height, which if practised will be found more difficult to get quite true than the network on mould No. 2.

The scroll work round the side is in the Rococo style, the pale yellow showing up well on the darker background. There are six panels at the base, each containing a small, neat, floral medallion, surrounded by small scrolling, which add considerably to the appearance of the whole. The mould is surmounted by a finely-piped hollow ball—one line built on the other, with the main colours heliotrope and yellow alternating.

The second mould shown is iced and piped in various shades of green, darker at the base and shading off until it is so pale at the top as to appear almost white. The pillar's top and ball are covered in fine network, shaded lighter towards the top, and the Gothic arches are well brought out. But the beauty of this particular mould is the large scroll round the side, and it is brought out in strong relief in the illustration. The panels contain medallions on which are piped lilies of the valley, maidenhair fern, etc., which complete a pretty and effective mould.

Note.—When choosing new moulds for Savoys, it is well to select those whose shape lends itself to easy cleaning and greasing, as the waste of time necessary to prepare some intricate moulds is not warranted by the price of the finished article.

SECTION VIII.

MERINGUE

PERHAPS this may be considered one of the favourite mixtures both of the confectioner and of the public. In some form or other it always finds a ready sale amongst almost all classes of the community. It can in turn be used for large halfpenny or penny goods, and what is important, it can show a good margin of profit. It can also be used for the smallest and neatest of fancies suitable for any buffet at afternoon tea or garden party.

We will give a few general rules for making meringue; every confectioner probably knows them, but for the benefit of the beginners they are given, for without attention to these main facts failure is sure to attend the efforts. Let every utensil be scrupulously clean, not a spot of dirt or grease anywhere; even after the assistant has washed the bowls and whisks, it is a good thing to scald them again. It is a wise plan to keep a good whisk and bowl to use solely for meringue, there will then be no fear of them being greasy. The same might be said as regards spoons, bags, tubes, etc., although with these it is not so important, as they are used after the whites are knocked up. Good whites should be used, not too fresh nor yet too stale. Fairly strong whites that have been separated for a day or two are the best. The reason for this is that a good deal of the moisture of the whites evaporates, leaving the albumen stronger than before and more likely to make a stiffer snow. Very fresh whites are apt to curdle or bruise if not beaten very carefully; when these are being used, a small handful of sugar put in before beating, or a drop of acid, will help to avert the curdling, and then a good steady, rather slow whisking at first, gradually getting faster, is the best way to treat them. If they are hurried at first they will probably curdle, with the result that the mixture will soon run back and be soft and unworkable.

SHELLS

Some shells are shown in the illustration in the right hand bottom corner. These should be made from equal quantities, *i.e.* to the whites of 1 lb. of eggs in shell take 1 lb. of good, clean castor sugar. Separate the whites into a clean bowl (which should be of a suitable size for free work with the whisk), and sift the sugar on a sheet of paper.

Whisk the whites to a snow, adding the sugar gradually, and beating in as much of it as possible. When well up, stir in the remainder of the sugar with a wooden spoon, place some of the mixture in a Savoy bag with a large plain tube, and lay out on greased and floured baking-sheets, somewhat in the shape of an egg. Dust

PIPED MERINGUES.

castor sugar over, place in a cool oven, and bake. They should take just the slightest colour. When done, mark the bottoms with a sharp-pointed knife, and either push the bottom in or remove the centre altogether, and put them in the prover or drying cupboard to dry. They are then ready to be filled with whipped cream and stuck together for sale. This is shown in the illustration. Many

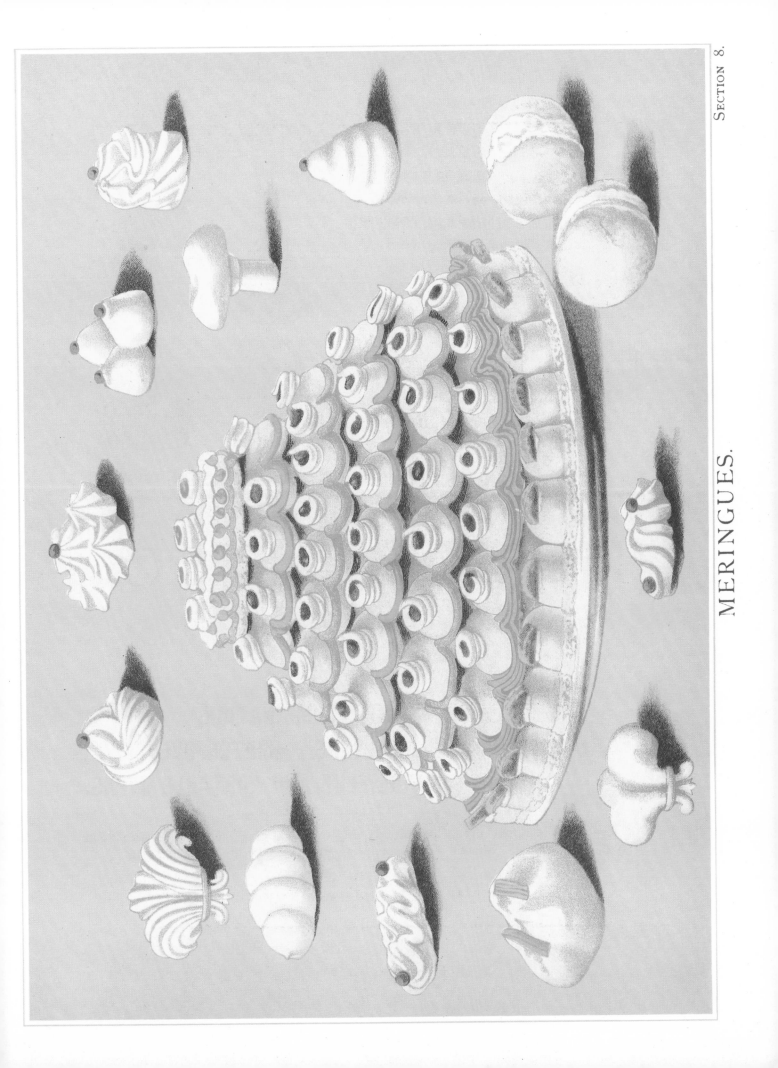

MERINGUES.

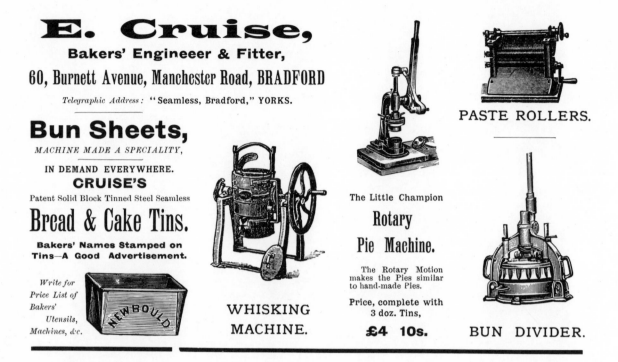

prefer to lay them out with a table-spoon, but this is a much slower method, and, to our mind, has nothing to recommend it.

The next two items are not illustrated, but are quite easy to make, and are good selling lines.

MASCOTTES

Use the whites and sugar in the same proportion as for shells, and proceed in exactly the same way as regards whisking. When finished, lay out in rather large finger shapes on prepared tins, sprinkle desiccated cokernut over, and bake in a cool oven. Half the number should be coloured pink.

PENNY MERINGUE GOODS

We give these as an example of the kind of goods that can be, and are, retailed in most shops at a penny, or even a halfpenny. Take the same mixing as before, and, when ready, place in a Savoy bag with large star pipe affixed, and form into horse-shoe shapes, thick and bold in the middle, and tapering to a point at each end. Sprinkle cobbled almonds over the whole and bake. The mixing can be laid out in numerous other fancy shapes.

MUSHROOMS

Knock the mixture well up, place a portion in the bag with a small medium tube and lay out the stalks. Then, with a rather larger size, lay out the meringue to represent the tops of the mushrooms. Bake, and colour the parts that should be dark with chocolate powder. An illustration of this pretty and saleable meringue fancy will be found amongst the others. Some still use the old-fashioned board and water both for these and other meringue goods, but it is considerably easier and better to use baking-sheets in nearly all instances.

On the same page are shown several illustrations of fancy meringues, but these need only little explanation. The mixture should not be too light, or they will be liable to blow and become ill-shaped. Six whites to the pound of sugar is sufficient. Beat in as much of the sugar as possible, and whisk well all the time. Lay out with plain and star tubes on greased and floured baking-sheets in the shapes shown.

BUILT MERINGUES

In the centre of the same page of illustrations is shown a fair example of built meringues. They were at one time greatly in vogue, but are not seen much now in actual business. They are usually made by forming rings of meringue of the required sizes, which are dried or baked, and afterwards placed on each other, sticking them together with the mixture. The whole should then be coated with meringue, much in the same manner as a cake is iced, and again dried. In the meantime a number of small pyramids or dots should be laid out and dried or baked. These should be stuck all over the shell, and then decorated by piping with meringue. Place on some silver dragees and similar aids to decoration. The centre should be filled with whipped cream if intended for table, but, as a rule, they seem to be made more for show than anything else, and we think that the time and labour might be more profitably employed on something that is really artistic.

SECTION IX.

MARZIPAN FLOWERS, FRUITS, &c., AND NOUGAT

THIS branch of artistic confectionery is one of the most interesting studies in the trade.

There is no more effective decoration for cake tops, medallions, etc., than roses and other flowers, if properly made and tastefully coloured; but there must be no mistake about either of these points. Unless marzipan roses are done well their place is in the practice-room, and not exposed to be admired. As in piping, no amount of writing will make a man a good flower modeller. Illustrations are given of roses of different sizes, a spray of mixed flowers, and a cake top with spray. These will give a good general idea of how well-modelled flowers should look, but any success is only to be obtained by constant practice and study. As this is practically an imitation of Nature, the learner cannot do better than go direct to Nature for his designs, and try to form flowers, petal by petal, as near in shape and lightness to the original as possible. Very good practice may be obtained by using modelling wax, or even the ordinary wax pared from a candle, and slightly warmed to make it pliable. Some people use a considerable number of utensils, such as small and fine palette knives, straight and curved scissors, and different shaped bone or ivory modelling tools; but for all practical purposes to the ordinary workman, the fingers are quite sufficient to get all the effects necessary.

The most convenient form of marzipan for rose and other flower making is that prepared and sold ready-made, as to make marzipan in the decorating-room would require a good set of granite rollers to make the paste sufficiently fine. Most of this prepared marzipan, if bought from a good firm, may be absolutely relied on, especially if the instructions as to storage, etc., sent by the respective makers are rigidly adhered to. Many of the recipes for the use of marzipan published and issued by most dealers will be found well worth trying. The first illustration shows a marzipan cake top decorated with flowers made of the same material. In Scotland these tops in various sizes are sometimes used for shortbread decoration, but in the opinion of the writers heavy almond work is out of place on shortbread. The base on which the flowers rest is moulded in a wooden block, such as are used sometimes for blocking shortbreads and gingerbreads. The flowers are arranged on the base into a pretty spray with leaves. (These latter may be purchased from any sundries-man.)

ROSES, &c.

1 lb. Marzipan Paste

1 lb. Fine Sifted Icing Sugar.

Work the paste and the sugar together until perfectly amalgamated and smooth. During this operation any colour

EXAMPLES OF DIFFERENT SIZED MARZIPAN ROSES.

required may be introduced, but care must be taken that the colouring is evenly distributed or the paste may be patchy or spotted. Take a small piece of the paste and roll out under hand until of about the size of a good-sized pencil. Break off

MARZIPAN FRUITS.

Exclusive—Artistic —and Low-priced !

**CAKE FRILLS,
GUM PASTE
ORNAMENTS,
WAFER ROSES,
DECORATIVE
NOVELTIES,
ARTIFICIAL
FLOWERS.**

Write for prices and particulars of Cake Boards, Bouquets and Vases, d'Oyles, Silver, Gold, and Frosted Leaves, Tier Stands, Flower Sprays, Wedding Cake Boxes, Side Ornaments, etc.

THERE is an immense advantage to be gained from ordering your Wedding Cake Ornaments and Cake Decorations from the U.Y.C. Our manufacturing equipment and specially trained staff enable us to catalogue a wide variety of exclusive lines at prices that really do save you money.

Every design is distinctive in appearance, artistic in its finish, and of first-rate workmanship and quality. We can supply instantly from stock any article and decoration that a baker is ever likely to require. Let the U.Y.C. give you this better value—coupled with a prompt and efficient service.

THE UNITED YEAST Co Ltd

80, Miller Street, Manchester ; 190, St. John Street, London, E.C.1 ; 103, Temple Street, Bristol ; :: Corporation Street, Newcastle ; Wellington Street & 15, Queen Street, Leeds ; Doe Street, Birmingham

2 or 3 inches and hold in the left hand. With the forefinger and thumb of the right hand press out the end of the paste into the shape of a rose petal. When this is satisfactorily done, and the edges are rolled as in the natural rose, cut off at a suitable

SPRAY OF MARZIPAN FLOWERS.

length and stand aside until three are done. These should be intertwined as for the centre bud of the rose, and further petals may be added in slightly varying sizes until the rose is complete.

Each petal is attached by slightly damping the bottom, and then pressing on at the required place. When well set, the rose may be mounted by sticking in a piece of wire (slightly heated) just at the place where the stalk would naturally grow.

Most colours may be made by mixing in as before described, but if dark red roses are required, they are better if painted with carmine powder.

The writers do not propose going on to describe the making of other flowers. Practice only can make proficient in marzipan roses or modelling of any description. Work on the lines briefly set out above, and follow Nature as much as possible.

MARZIPAN FRUITS

The advice given for making roses, etc., applies equally in the case of the forming of marzipan fruits. As the object is to get as near a representation of the real fruit as possible, no better pattern can be obtained, both of colour and of form and size, than a sample of the fruit itself. Take about 1 lb. marzipan (prepared) and work into it as much fine sifted icing sugar as possible, taking care that the paste when finished is not too dry, and consequently too brittle. The amount of sugar required should be

A MARZIPAN CAKE TOP.

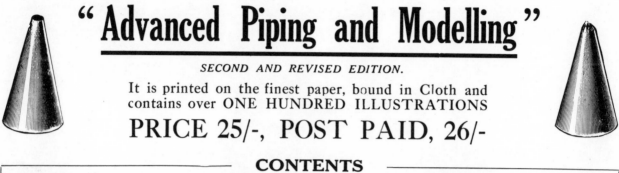

from $1\frac{1}{2}$ lbs. to 2 lbs., according to the quantity of moisture contained in the marzipan. Break off a piece of the paste of the required size and mould it with the hands into as exact a copy as possible of the fruit. The operation of colouring varies from that used for general flowers, in that, instead of colouring the paste throughout, powdered colours are used, and are applied to the fruit by "dabbing" it with cotton wool dipped in the powders. If it is found that any of the colours are too intense, they may be lightened by adding to the powder a small quantity of icing sugar or other white powder.

The bloom seen on grapes and dark plums may be imitated by very lightly touching the finished fruit with the slightest possible amount of white. An illustration is given of some good examples of fruits (plate 1, Section IX.).

NOUGAT

An illustration is given of a wheelbarrow made entirely of nougat and filled with marzipan roses. Nougat is more often used in kitchens than in bakehouses in England, and although it is common to meet chefs who are adepts at nougat work, it is decidedly the exception to meet a confectioner who knows any-

Y

thing about it. It is very useful indeed for making little baskets for holding cream and fruit, and for forming practically any style of piece montée.

WHEELBARROW IN NOUGAT FILLED WITH MARZIPAN FLOWERS.

    1 lb. Finely Chopped Almonds

    1 lb. Castor Sugar

    A few drops of Lemon Juice.

Put the sugar and lemon juice into a copper stew-pan and

put on stove or gas ring. Keep gently stirred with a wooden spoon until all the sugar is melted, then throw the almonds in and stir until well mixed. The paste is then ready for use, and should be turned out on a slightly oiled slab, rolled out, and formed into any design required. To make small baskets, etc., it is only necessary to line some small moulds, slightly oiled, with the rolled-out nougat, carefully trimming the edges before the paste sets, as afterwards it becomes very brittle. Handles to the baskets may be made with sugar as described in Section X., page 176.

SECTION X.

CHARLOTTE ECOSSAISE AND TRIFLE

THESE two articles do not quite come in the category of "cakes," but, as they are often in request from confectioners and are not over difficult to make, they are included in this work.

CHARLOTTE ECOSSAISE

Prepare a Charlotte mould by thoroughly cleaning it (absolute cleanliness is essential). Take a number of quite evenly made sponge-fingers, and dip into very hot pink fondant. For variety it is expedient to divide the fingers into three equal lots, and to dip one lot into chocolate fondant, another into white, and the last into pink. These are then used in rotation. Each finger should be tested to see that it accurately fits the mould when put to stand round upright as a lining. Cut a piece of paper to fit the bottom of mould and place in position so that when ready to turn out there may be no difficulty. Prepare a cream from the following recipe, paying particular attention to every detail :—

1 pint Milk

$\frac{1}{4}$ lb. Sugar

4 Yolks of Eggs

1 oz. of Sheet Gelatine (fine and white)

$\frac{1}{2}$ pint of Cream.

Put the milk in a good saucepan on the fire to boil. Thoroughly beat up the yolks and sugar in a bowl, and when the milk boils, pour the mixture into the saucepan, quickly stirring until the custard begins to thicken, when it should be lifted off the fire. The gelatine, which has been previously well soaked, should be now stirred in, and the hot custard speedily dissolves it. Pass through a sieve, and set aside to cool. Whilst this is cooling, whisk the cream up stiff, and when the custard is cool enough without being cold, beat together with the cream. When the mixture is nearly setting, it must be quickly filled into the sponge-lined mould and put aside to get quite hard. There should be very little difficulty in turning the Charlotte out of the mould if the fingers have been well arranged and if the custard was stiff enough before being put in. If the custard is too soft or warm, or if the fingers are far apart so that the filling may ooze through, the Charlotte will stick to the mould, and its appearance will be damaged. When turned out, strip the paper off the top, and place the Charlotte on a glass stand. Take some thick cream with a little sugar and whip up stiff. Divide, and make into the desired colours, which must be filled into bags fitted with star pipes. Pipe all round the bottom edge on the stand to form lower border, and with a smaller tube, pipe a star design in colours to cover the whole of the top. The decoration may be completed by piping the sides with whites icing, coloured to blend with the fondants, if thought desirable, angelica and silver dragees may be used as shown in the illustration.

CHARLOTTE ECOSSAISE

ANOTHER METHOD

This is more simple than the last, and can be done much more quickly. Mask the fingers with fondant, pipe, and finish them off. Mould the cream as given in No. 1 in a Charlotte mould and set aside to get cold. When ready to turn out, dip in hot water and turn out smartly on a glass stand. The fingers will then readily adhere to the wet sides, and as the cream dries will become quite firm. The top and border may then be finished as before directed.

CHARLOTTE RUSSE

THIS is somewhat similar to the Charlotte Ecossaise, but is not so ornate, and consequently does not take so long to make. Charlotte Russe may be made in any shaped Charlotte mould, but it probably looks at its best in the ordinary oval mould sold for the purpose. Prepare the mould by thoroughly cleaning. Run about $\frac{1}{4}$ inch of bright, clear jelly into the bottom, taking care that it does not splash about the sides. The jelly may be decorated with a design in fruit and pistachios before setting, or by piping with another coloured jelly after setting. Place round the sides of mould to form a lining, a sufficient number of plain, even, Savoy fingers, and set aside for the jelly to set. When the jelly is quite firm, fill the mould up with the cream and custard, mixing as directed for Charlotte Ecossaise, and place in the cool until the whole is firm. This will readily turn out, and may be served in a silver dish or on a glass stand. A variety in Charlotte Russe may be obtained by cutting out, from some sheets of sponge, fingers in different colours, which may be placed close together, either upright or slanted, the colours being, of course, used alternately.

TRIFLE

THE illustration gives a fair idea of a flat trifle, somewhat elaborated by the pulled sugar handle, and the spun sugar on the cherries. Commence by soaking with syrup and sherry, in a glass dish, some jam roll, or stale sponge cake, jammed. When the cake is well saturated, pour off most of the spare moisture which lies in the bottom of the dish. Whip some cream up very stiff, add a little sugar, and with this cover the whole of the cake, making the top of a rocky appearance, by dropping small spoonfuls of cream on. This trifle is then practically finished. To decorate as in illustration, take some crescent-shaped macaroons and place round as shown, they will stick up in the cream, or lightly wedged between glass and cream. Place a cherry, which has been covered with spun sugar, on the top of each biscuit. The handle is made of pulled or twisted sugar, and this operation needs some little practice. We give below the method by which it is made, but practice only will bring a measure of success.

> 2 lbs. Sugar (Cane Loaf)
> $\frac{1}{2}$ pt. Water
> A little Glucose.

Trifle.

Charlotte Eccossais.

Boil the sugar to the crack degree, and divide into separate vessels, one for each colour required. Pour out on a slab which has been prepared by lightly rubbing over with oil, and wait until the sugar commences to cool. Do not wait long, but directly the first fierce heat has gone off, take a palette knife and quickly fold the sides of the sugar over into the middle, and continue this until the mixing is just cool enough to handle. Then take up the sugar in your oiled hands, and draw out to about a foot long, slightly twisting it as you pull. Put the ends of the string together and draw out again, and continue this until the sugar looks like shining satin, and is beginning to get cool, when it must at once be formed into whatever design is required. For the handle in this trifle, all that would be necessary would be to lay out a long string of pulled and twisted sugar on the slab in the shape illustrated, and when cold this would be hard and brittle. The little pink "tie ups" are done in the same way with the pink sugar. After fixing the handle, petals of crystallised flowers are stuck on with sugar, and a piped rose is fastened on the top.

MACAROON TRIFLE

THE usual way of making trifle is the following, and it has the advantage over the previous method of being more imposing in appearance when served on the table as a cold sweet.

Take a stale, tall sponge cake (moulded), slice it in several places and jam it, carefully replacing it in its former position, and soak it well with syrup and sherry. This should be done on the day before the trifle is required, to ensure its being well saturated. Place it in a trifle dish, and pour over all the liquor which has not been absorbed overnight. Strew a quantity of ratafias and broken macaroons all round the base of sponge, and pour over all the following custard, which should completely cover everything :—

> 1 pint of Milk
>
> ¼ lb. Sugar
>
> 4 Yolks of Eggs.

Boil the milk in a saucepan, and, whilst doing so, beat up

the sugar and yolks. When the milk boils, quickly pour in the other ingredients and stir briskly for a few minutes, when it is ready for use.

The dish may now be set aside for the custard to cool, and the time may be occupied by whisking up a sufficient quantity of cream with a little sugar to cover the custard. This may be done when the custard is quite cold. The best way of putting on the cream is to throw it on with a spoon, thus giving it a rocky appearance. This completes the trifle, but it may be decorated by sprinkling the top with finely chopped pistachios or tiny comfits, and the base may be lightly strewn with small bits of coloured rock sugar.

SECTION XI.

POUND AND SLAB CAKES

THE trade in pound and slab cakes appears during the past few years to have been somewhat neglected by the confectionery trade, which has not kept pace with the progressive factories that have sprung up in many districts for the manufacture and distribution of this class of confectionery. There seems little doubt that, in the long run, if more attention is paid to this line, the business will revert into its proper channels; but the close study of this branch by confectioners is the only means by which this result may be attained.

Our object at this time will be to point out the best means of doing this trade to the advantage both of the tradesman and of the public. In the first place it is necessary to be very particular about the use of ingredients. Everything must be good, sweet, and wholesome. Careful attention must be paid to flour, sugar, eggs, butter or other fat, fruit, moisture, chemicals and flavourings. Flour for cakes must be carefully selected, so that it may be sufficiently strong without being so strong that the even vesiculation of the cake is spoiled, and it should be of a good flavour and colour. A good blend of Hungarian and British milled is suitable for best goods, though for cheaper cakes a small quantity of Spring or Winter Patent American may be mixed instead of the Vienna flour. See that all flour is well sifted and blended before use. The question of sugar has been treated in the chapter on materials, and needs no further comment. Great care should be taken in the breaking and examination of eggs; each egg should be broken into a vessel by itself before adding to the bulk of those already broken, as a few spots of the white of a musty egg are sufficient to taint a decent-sized mixing. It seems in some quarters to be considered smart to break out the eggs at a great pace, but a little time is well expended in careful breaking, both as regards better examination and the increased weight of whites obtained by wiping out the shell with the finger. Butter, before use for creaming up, should be well worked under hand to get rid of moisture, and to make the whole of the same consistency. In cases in which the butter is too salt (a little salt is an advantage) it may be found necessary to give it a thorough washing, and if there is any doubt about the quantity of salt this should be done. Fruit must be well cleaned. Nothing is more objectionable than for a customer to constantly come across grit, bits of stem, and even stones in a fruit cake. Currants should be washed in several waters, or one of the many good machines sold for the purpose may be used. In the first instance, the currants should be well rubbed in a fruit sieve to get rid of a proportion of stems, etc., and after being washed may be laid out to dry. When dried sufficiently, they should be carefully hand picked before being ready for use. A good way to pick fruit is the old method of taking an ordinary baking sheet, and placing some pounds of currants at one end, then with the fingers of both hands quickly scoop them a few at a time to the other end of the tin. Any stones which escape the eye will in this way easily be heard as they scrape on the iron.

Moisture, which usually consists of milk, needs no remarks, except that in the country where fresh buttermilk can be obtained, it will be found economical and otherwise expedient to use it.

Chemicals should be thoroughly mixed and sifted with the flour. Put the mixture through the sieve several times, as nothing is more unsightly in a cake than to see brown spots caused by small unmixed bits of soda bicarbonate. In many bakeries and kitchens, what is called patent flour is used instead of mixing the chemicals for each separate batch of cakes. This is made in several strengths, but the following will be found reliable, and will be used in some of the recipes in this section :—

> 21 lbs. Good Flour
>
> 7 ozs. Cream of Tartar
>
> 4 ozs. Bicarbonate of Soda.

Thoroughly mix and sift as before directed. Carbonate of ammonia, tartaric acid, and other chemicals are sometimes used, but they do not require to be touched on here.

There is no intention in offering the following recipes and methods as being anything original, either in names or quantities. The cakes described have been, for the most part, sold under these names for years; but we do offer them as reliable recipes which have been well tested and which will be found trustworthy and profitable.

BAKING POWDER

Where powder is mentioned in the following recipes use—

> 2 lbs. Cream of Tartar
>
> 1 lb. Bicarbonate of Soda.

Prepare by carefully sifting several times through a fine sieve, and keep in a dry canister for use as required.

Methods of Working Recipes

In creaming up butter and sugar, do not grudge hard work: at this stage of manufacture the tendency is to give insufficient work, with the result that the lightness of the cake is impaired. Eggs must be beaten in a small quantity at a time, taking care that the mixture does not curdle; if any signs of curdling are noticed, a portion of the previously weighed flour should be beaten in, and this will make it smooth and allow the rest of the eggs to be added.

Essences and Flavours.—The ideas of many in the trade do not rise above the level of the essences of lemon and vanilla, and these are used in season and out of season. A mixing is never considered complete unless it has had the contents of the essence bottle shaken into it, whether it wants it or not. This is certainly not as it should be Essence is not an invariable ingredient in any cake recipe and should only be used for the purpose of importing a distinctive flavour. Learned treatises have been written giving elaborate chemical prescriptions for flavouring each separate kind of cake, but if the flour, butter, sugar, and fruit are good, very little artificial flavour is required. We know of one prominent high-class cake house, in the bakery of which lemon essence is strictly tabooed. Not because this particular flavouring is bad, but because the British confectioner, if he can see the bottle, will use it. For delicate gateaux, fillings, etc., the best flavourings are the finest liqueurs procurable.

We now come to the question as to what utensils are required for pound and slab cake. Many machines have been invented and are on the market for creaming up purposes, and some few profess to beat in the eggs and mix in the flour and fruit. Without in any way suggesting any make of machine to the probable buyer, we would advise him to see every machine advertised for the purpose, and choose the one which does the work best.   Nothing is gained by laying down cheap machinery because it is low priced.   Good materials and workmanship in bakery machines are essential and they must be paid for at a fair rate.   The same remarks apply to ovens, sponge beaters, peel cutters, almond machines, and indeed to all the utensils that a confectioner needs.   Strong block-tin hoops and tins must be used for baking, as the cheap thin ones so soon buckle and come out of shape.   Wooden frames for slab cake must be made of well-seasoned wood from $\frac{5}{8}$ inch to $\frac{7}{8}$ inch thick.   In the preparation of tins, hoops, and frames, it is necessary to see that they are perfectly clean, and that the paper bands when used lie close to the side of the hoop, so that there may be no pulling out of shape in the oven.

FRUIT GENOA SLAB (1)

$1\frac{1}{2}$ lbs. Butter

$1\frac{1}{2}$ lbs. Sugar

2 lbs. Flour

$\frac{1}{2}$ lb. Patent Flour

2 lbs. Eggs

$1\frac{1}{2}$ lbs. Sultanas

$1\frac{1}{2}$ lbs. Currants

$1\frac{1}{2}$ lbs. Peel.

Cream up the butter and sugar, and beat in the eggs, stir in the flour and fruit, and fill into papered tins or wood frames. Coarsely chopped almonds should be plentifully sprinkled on top of each cake, which should then be baked in a sound oven.   It is most important to study the heat of the oven when making cakes, slab cakes in particular. Experience is the only reliable teacher of the proper temperatures, as ovens, pyrometers, and thermometers vary considerably. It is a common error to try and bake slab cakes in a really cool oven, and the results are ofttimes nearly as disastrous as in the case of the other extreme. What should be aimed at is a good solid oven, with nothing flash in the heat, but which will keep a moderately sound temperature during the baking. It is then well to remember that to a great extent the success of successful slab cake-making lies in the baking.

FRUIT SLAB GENOA (2)

This is more fruity than No. 1, and is in all respects a most saleable cake :—

4 lbs. Butter
4 lbs. Sugar
2 quarts Eggs
5 lbs. Flour
8 lbs. Currants
4 lbs. Sultanas
3 lbs. Peel
1 lb. Cherries
1 lb. Whole Almonds.
Method as No. 1.

This cake should be baked with chopped almonds sprinkled on top, unless, as is often the case, it is to be covered with almond paste, for which, of course, the top is left plain.

PLAIN GENOA OR BEST RICE

4 lbs. Butter
4½ lbs. Sugar
4 lbs. Eggs
5 lbs. Flour
½ lb. Ground Rice
Bare ½ oz. Powder
½ pt. Milk.

Cream up the butter and sugar, beat in the eggs a few at a time, and then carefully mix in the flour, ground rice and milk. The powder has, of course, been previously carefully sifted through the flour.

This mixing turns out an excellent plain cake, which cuts firmly, without being cloggy.

GENOA SEED OR SULTANA SLAB

The following mixing may be used for either Seed or Sultana, and is very popular on account of its excellent eating qualities :—

6 lbs. Butter
6 lbs. Sugar
2 quarts Eggs
7 lbs. Flour
4 ozs. Ground Almonds.

For Seed Cake add 4 oz. Caraway Seeds.
For Sultana Cake add 6 lbs. Sultanas.

Cream up the butter and sugar, and add in the ground almonds. Beat in the eggs slowly and stir in the flour, seeds, or fruit.   Before baking, the top of this cake may be sprinkled with flaked or chipped almonds.

CHERRY CAKE

$3\frac{1}{2}$ lbs. Butter

$3\frac{1}{2}$ lbs. Sugar

3 pts. Eggs

$4\frac{1}{2}$ lbs. Flour

Bare $\frac{1}{2}$ oz. Powder

$3\frac{1}{2}$ lbs. Cherries

$1\frac{1}{2}$ lbs. Citron.

Cream up butter and sugar, add the eggs, and stir in flour, fruit, etc., in the usual way. The cherries may either be used whole or chopped; the former looks much better and is advised. If the cherries carry an excess of syrup, it is well to wash them in warm water and slightly dry them in a cloth; this will often prevent the cherries falling to the bottom, and will always prevent the cake becoming stained from the syrup. Citron looks best cut in small cubes about $\frac{3}{4}$ of the size of a cherry.

SLAB FRUIT CAKE

This cake should be sold at about 8d. per lb., but the price must be regulated by the quality of materials used.

3 lbs. Butter or good mixture

$4\frac{1}{2}$ lbs. Sugar

4 lbs. Eggs

6 lbs. flour

        1 oz. powder
        4 lbs. Currants
        4 lbs. Sultanas
        2 lbs. Peel
        About 1 pt. Milk.

Cream up butter and sugar, add the eggs slowly. Stir in flour (sifted with the powder) and fruit. Bake in sound oven.

SLAB SEED

This is the seed companion to above mixing and should be also sold at about 8d. per lb.

        $2\frac{1}{2}$ lbs. Butter or good mixture
        $2\frac{1}{2}$ lbs. Sugar
        $2\frac{1}{2}$ lbs. Eggs
        5 lbs. Flour
        1 oz. Powder
        $2\frac{1}{2}$ ozs. Caraway Seeds
        Milk.

Cream up butter and sugar, add eggs by beating in slowly, stir in flour and seeds.

SLAB SULTANA FRUIT CAKE

(CHEAPER QUALITY)

        5 lbs. Mixture
        5 lbs. Sugar
        5 lbs. Eggs

10 lbs. Flour
2 ozs. Powder
6 lbs. Sultanas
2 lbs. Peel
Milk.

Cream up mixture and sugar, add eggs as in a best mixing, and stir in flour, fruit, milk, etc. This cake may be sold retail at 6d. per lb., and is a good competitive line.

SLAB FRUIT CAKE

(CHEAP)

This class of cake has often to be made in competition, and although it is not a very desirable line, it must nowadays be included in any cake book.

11 lbs. Flour
3 ozs. Powder
2½ lbs. Mixture
5 lbs. Sugar
3 qts. Milk (bare)
7½ lbs. Fruit.

This is a creamed-up mixing, and should be done in exactly the same way as better quality cakes, but may with advantage be baked in a somewhat hotter oven.

This completes the different ordinary grades of slab cakes; varieties and novelties may be made by any practical man when working the foregoing recipes. As an example:—a cake is sometimes made with a layer of almond paste running through the middle; this can easily be done by taking one of the better fruit slab mixings, and introducing the paste into the centre at the time of filling the tins or frames. Cakes may be cheapened or otherwise by decreasing or increasing the more expensive ingredients, always taking care to counteract any alteration in eggs by a corresponding alteration in powder and moisture.

POUND CAKES

The generally accepted meaning of the term pound cake is usually a cake made of the following recipe:—

1 lb. Butter
1 lb. Sugar
1 lb. Eggs
1 lb. Flour
1 lb. Fruit.

But we propose using the term to cover all that class of cakes which are usually sold in round tins—uncut—as distinct from slab cakes, school cakes and plum bread. The appearance of cakes of this kind if the mixture is right, depends largely on the finish, both as regards baking, and papers or bands. These bands should always be carefully put in the tins or hoops, so that, when weighing in, the mixture is not smeared on the band. Care should also be exercised that the band is not too high for the cake, for if so, the upper edge of the paper becomes either charred, or so brittle that the appearance is soon spoilt by chipping and cracking.

A good composite cake mixing which may be split up into

various kinds during manufacture is given below. A portion
may be weighed off plain for Madeira Cake, to another part
may be added a few cherries for Cherry Cake, to a third part
may be added seeds for Seed Cake, whilst to the last a few
currants added will make a good fruit pound. In each case
take care that too much fruit is not added.

> 3 lbs. Butter
> 3 lbs. Sugar
> 4 lbs. Eggs
> 4 lbs. Flour
> $\frac{1}{4}$ oz. Powder.

If the flour is very dry a little moisture may be added.
Cream up the butter and sugar very thoroughly, as otherwise
the eggs may curdle. Beat in the eggs a few at a time; stir
in the flour, etc. Thin slices of citron peel may be placed on
the top of the Madeira cakes, which should be baked in a sound
oven.

MADEIRA CAKE

> 2 lbs. Butter
> $2\frac{1}{4}$ lbs. Sugar
> $2\frac{1}{2}$ lbs. Eggs
> $2\frac{1}{2}$ lbs. Flour
> A few spots of Madeira Essence.

Cream up butter and sugar, beat in the whites of eggs, after
which the yolks and essence may be stirred in. Mix in the
flour. Weigh into round papered hoops and dredge with sugar.
Place on top two slices of citron peel and bake in a sound oven.

MADEIRA CAKE

(Cheap)

This mixing may be used for sixpenny or penny Madeiras.

> 1 lb. Sugar
> 10 ozs. Butter or Mixture
> 6 Eggs
> 2 lbs. Patent Flour
> $\frac{1}{2}$ pint Milk
> A few drops Lemon Essence.

Cream up the butter and sugar and add the eggs. Mix in the flour, milk, and flavouring. Dredge with sugar, and bake in quite a warm oven.

POUND GENOA CAKE

This cake looks exceedingly well if baked in long, shallow oval tins, papered in the usual way.

> 2 lbs. Butter
> 2 lbs. Sugar
> 3 lbs. Eggs
> 3 lbs. Flour
> 1 lb. Sultanas
> $\frac{1}{2}$ lb. Peel (finely chopped).

Cream up in the usual way, and beat in the eggs, taking care that the mixing does not curdle. Add flour and fruit, and fill into tins. Sprinkle coarsely cut almonds on top, dredge with sugar, and bake in moderately warm oven.

DUNDEE CAKE (1)

2 lbs. Butter
2 lbs. Sugar
$2\frac{1}{2}$ lbs. Eggs
3 lbs. Flour
$\frac{1}{2}$ lb. Patent Flour
2 lbs. Currants
1 lb. Sultanas
$1\frac{1}{2}$ lbs. Peel
Lemon Essence.

Cream up the butter and sugar, add the eggs and mix in the fruit, essence and flour. If the mixing is not free enough, a few drops of milk may be added. Fill into round hoops or tins and sprinkle whole almonds over the top.

DUNDEE CAKE (2)

2 lbs. Butter
2 lbs. Sugar
$3\frac{1}{2}$ lbs. Eggs
4 lbs. Flour
$\frac{1}{2}$ oz. Carbonate Soda
$\frac{1}{2}$ oz. Tartaric Acid
1 lb. Currants
1 lb. Sultanas
1 lb. Peel
$\frac{1}{2}$ lb. Almonds.

Proceed as before, and finish in the same way. This is a very old mixing, slightly antagonistic to present methods in the way of powder, but withal a good serviceable and saleable article.

2 B

POUND SULTANA CAKE

2½ lbs. Butter

2½ lbs. Sugar

22 Eggs

3 lbs. Flour

1 lb. Patent Flour

3 lbs. Sultanas

1 lb. Peel.

Cream up butter and sugar and beat in the eggs. Mix in the fruit and flour and fill into round papered hoops. Two slices of citron peel should be placed on top before baking in a moderate oven.

As in the case of the slab cakes, the foregoing recipes may be altered and varied to suit particular requirements. We have abstained from giving either prices for selling, or weights for making, as in different districts different prices are bound to obtain. All cakes should be made on a system, and very little deviation allowed in relative quantities of fat and sugar. Lightness in cakes may be obtained by the use of either eggs or powder, and sufficient of either or both must be employed to lighten the amount of flour used.

SCHOOL CAKES

School Cake, which is sometimes called "Currant Bread" or "Plum Bread," is a very favourite article at school tea parties, etc. The cake may be made of any quality, but the usual price at which it is sold varies from 4d. to 6d. per lb.

We shall give recipes for those, together with others for which more money may be asked. It is usual to bake school cakes of all kinds in ordinary quartern or half quartern tins, although sometimes they are in request, baked in "yards" or long sandwich bread tins.

SCHOOL CAKE (1)

This cake is above the 6d. limit, but is an exceedingly good school cake which often takes the place of a luncheon pound.

3 lbs. Butter or Mixture
3 lbs. Sugar
1 quart Eggs
3 lbs. Flour
3 lbs. Patent Flour
3 lbs. Sultanas
2 lbs. Currants
$\frac{3}{4}$ lb. Peel
Few drops Essence of Lemon
Milk.

Cream up mixture as for pound cakes, and fill into square or oblong tins (previously greased). Two pieces of cut citron peel may be put on top.

SCHOOL CAKE (2)

This is a much cheaper cake than the last.
1$\frac{1}{2}$ lbs. Mixture
2 lbs. Sugar

6 Eggs
7 lbs. Patent Flour
Fruit as required
Essence of Lemon
Milk.

Cream up the butter and sugar, and add the eggs. Mix in the essence, flour, and fruit, and add sufficient milk to make it of the proper consistency. This cake should be mixed fairly soft. Fill into square and oblong tins, dredge with sugar, and bake in a medium warm oven.

SCHOOL CAKE (3)

This is given as a cheaper variety which may be used in competition and can be cheapened to practically any degree. It is, as will be seen, a very plain cake, but turns out of a smart appearance, and is very useful for cheap contract work.

8 lbs. Patent Flour
$1\frac{1}{2}$ lbs. Mixture or Lard
$1\frac{1}{4}$ lbs. Sugar
4 lbs. Currants
1 lb. Peel
2 quarts Milk.

As this mixing does not contain much fat and is quite devoid of eggs, the creaming-up process is dispensed with and the fat is rubbed into the flour. When this has been done thoroughly, make a bay, and put the sugar inside and the fruit on the outside. Pour the milk into the bay, and if desired, a few spots of egg yellow, thoroughly mix, and fill into oblong tins of the size required. Lightly dredge on top and bake thoroughly.

COMPOSITE CAKE

This is a recipe that may be used in making many varieties of sixpenny cakes. The mixing is made up plain, and then divided into as many parts as sorts are required. For Currant Cake add currants, for Sultana Cake add sultanas, for Cocoanut Cake add desiccated cokernut, for Seed Cake add caraway seeds, etc. etc. This mixture should make seven cakes, which should be baked in oblong tins without papers :—

$\frac{1}{2}$ lb. Butter
1 lb. Sugar
6 Eggs
2 lbs. Flour
$1\frac{1}{2}$ ozs. Powder
1 pt. Milk.

Cream up the butter and sugar, beat in the eggs, and mix in the flour, powder, and milk. As this cake has rather a lot of powder in proportion, it will stand the necessary knocking about to work in the other fruits, etc. The cakes should be finished by sprinkling a few currants on the top of currant cakes, cokernut on cocoanut, and so on. A hot oven is required to bake these cakes to perfection

SECTION XII.

SPONGE AND MISCELLANEOUS CAKES

FOR the proper manufacture of sponge goods of all descriptions, in any quantity, a good machine sponge beater is required. There are many reliable machines on the market, which may be driven by power—steam, gas, or electrical; the smaller sizes, of course, being turned by hand.

PENNY SPONGES

4 lbs. Eggs
3½ lbs. Sugar
3 lbs. Flour.

Put the sugar to warm on a tray near the oven. Break the eggs carefully and put into the machine. Sift the flour on paper on the board ready for use. Start the machine, and pour the sugar in on the eggs. This must be well beaten until the mixture has considerably increased in volume, and is so thick that it does not readily run off the beaters. Remove the beaters, or pour the mixing out into a bowl, and lightly stir in the flour, giving it no more work than is necessary to thoroughly mix the flour and batter. Fill into sponge frames, either with a Savoy bag, by hand, or with a spoon, the latter is advised. Dredge over with sugar and bake in a moderately warm oven. When baked, turn out at once on a rack or other receptacle.

To Prepare Sponge Frames

This is of such importance that a few directions are necessary. Well-finished sponge cakes cannot be made unless the frames are properly prepared, and many good-sized mixings have been partially spoiled by carelessness in getting the tins ready, resulting in broken and badly scarred cakes, and dirty corners. Many fantastic methods have been advised for preparing these frames, but it is quite unnecessary to go further than the old method, briefly set out here. Well brush out the frames with a clean hard brush kept solely for the purpose. Put a quantity of lard into a clean tin, and warm until it is soft enough to paint with, then with a small brush quickly paint the insides of the frames with the fat, so that every bit of tin is covered with a very thin layer of white fat. When the lard is just in the right condition, the most casual examination will reveal any carelessness. Have ready on the board a quantity of sifted fine sugar, and an equal quantity of sifted flour, in two separate heaps. Fill the greased frames with sugar and shake out again, it will be found that the sugar attaching to the lard has made a casing or lining to the frame. The frame must then be filled with flour in the same way, and shaken out. To get rid of any superfluity of sugar or flour, it is as well to give the frame, held top downwards, a smart blow on the edge of the board. As a matter of expediency, in some bakeries, the flour and sugar are sifted together and are used at one operation. Good results may be obtained this way, but for the ordinary man who desires the best finished articles, the old method has yet to be beaten.

SPONGE FINGERS OR SAVOY BISCUITS

$1\frac{1}{2}$ lbs. Eggs, less 2 whites
$1\frac{1}{4}$ lbs. Sugar
$1\frac{1}{4}$ lbs. Flour.

Put the eggs and sugar into the sponge machine and beat up until thick. When ready, remove the beaters, and gently stir in the flour by hand until it is thoroughly mixed, being careful not to give too much work at this stage. Fill the mixture into a Savoy bag with a medium tube, and lay out in fingers of the required length on ordinary kitchen paper. Dredge well all over with fine sugar, and in a few minutes take up the paper in the hands by the two corners, and in this way allow all superfluous sugar to fall off on the board. Place the sheet on a baking-sheet and bake in a warm oven. When cooked, turn face downward on the board, and brush the back with a watery brush. In a few minutes the biscuits may be easily removed and stuck together in pairs.

BISCUIT A LA CUILLÈRE

This is practically the French equivalent of our Savoy Finger.

2 lbs. Eggs
1 lb. Sugar
1 lb. Flour.

Separate the whites from the yolks. Beat the sugar and yolks together with two whites, until it becomes a nice thick cream. Whisk the remainder of the whites up firm as for meringue.

Sift the flour into the yolks and sugar, and lightly mix the whole together. Finish as directed for Savoy fingers, except that the biscuits are laid out much longer, and that after being dredged they are slightly splashed with water, which raises small light bubbles on the sugar. This mixing requires considerable care. It is very light and may easily be spoiled by insufficient work in the earlier stages or by too much mixing in the later stages. It is, however, an excellent biscuit, but seldom met with to perfection in this country.

SWISS ROLL

This article, otherwise called Jam Roll, Jelly Roll, and many other names, is a standard selling line in every confectioner's business. Most people have their own mixing for this, and the following is given as being thoroughly reliable, easily worked, and as in every way turning out a first-class roll.

> 5 pints of Eggs
> 4½ lbs. Sugar
> 4 lbs. Flour
> Jam.

Put the eggs, carefully broken, into the machine. Warm the sugar and pour into the eggs. Whisk well up until the mixture is thick and creamy. When the batter shows little inclination to drop off the beaters, it is ready. Then take out of machine, and lightly, but thoroughly, mix in the sifted flour. Spread on papered and greased baking-sheets. Make as even as possible with a palette knife, and bake in a sound oven until of a nice bright colour.

Do not allow to cook too much, or the sheet of sponge may be difficult to roll. Turn over on a cloth or clean sack and remove paper. Spread all over, evenly, whatever kind of jam is required, and roll up fairly tight. The roll is then ready for sale, but if it is desired it may be lightly washed with water and rolled in sugar, or fine cokernut. Care should be taken to see that the jam is smooth. Raspberry does not, as a rule, require any preparation. But apricot jam and greengage jam will usually require sieving, *i.e.* passing through a coarse hair sieve.

VICTORIA OR JAM SANDWICH

These are baked in the tins sold for the purpose. Prepare the tins by greasing well and then dusting out with sifted flour. This mixing makes about six of the deep pans (usual size) or twelve of the shallow ones.

> 1 lb. 2 ozs. Sugar
> 1½ lbs. Eggs
> 1 lb. 4 ozs. Flour
> Pinch of Powder or Carbonate of Ammonia.

Thoroughly beat up the sugar and eggs in machine. When this is thick enough to hold to the wires of the beater, turn out in a bowl and lightly mix in the flour, into which has already been sifted the powder. Fill into the sandwich tins, and bake in a moderately hot oven. As this mixing contains powder in addition to a fair number of eggs, it is well not to disturb them until they are cooked, or they may sag in the middle. When cool, slice the deep ones through the middle and spread with jam.

In the case of the shallow ones, two may be stuck together with jam, giving practically the same effect.

SHILLING AND SIXPENNY SPONGE CAKES

These cakes are usually baked in square or oblong tins, and are sometimes called "Diet" cakes. The tins must be prepared in the same way as for penny sponges.

> 2 lbs. Eggs
> 2 lbs. Sugar
> 2 lbs. Flour.

Break the eggs and put them into the machine with the sugar which has been previously slightly warmed. Start the machine and beat thoroughly until the bulk has increased considerably, and until the batter will retain impressions for some little time. Turn out of machine and mix in the sifted flour by hand. Do not beat the mixing after the flour has been added, or the lightness may be impaired. Fill into suitably-sized tins, not more than five-eighths full, and dredge slightly in the middle. Bake in a moderate oven. If there is too much bottom heat in the oven, it is well to prevent burning by placing the tins containing the cakes into other tins of about the same size and thus baking them.

GATEAU WITH MARZIPAN ROSES.
The base is made of Genoese, sliced and butter creamed.

ANGEL CAKE

This cake needs no introduction or description. We do not know if this is or is not the inventor's recipe, but if properly worked it turns out a somewhat similar article.

1 pt. Whites
$1\frac{1}{4}$ lbs. Sugar
$\frac{3}{4}$ lb. Flour
$\frac{1}{4}$ oz. Cream of Tartar
Little Salt
Essence of Vanilla.

Whisk the whites in a clean vessel, until they are stiff (as for meringue), add the sugar by degrees, still beating. Stir in the flour with powder sifted in, very lightly. The salt should be put in the whites. These cakes were originally baked in special tins, which allowed of a ring up the centre of cake, but they may be made in any round or oval-shaped tin, if it is not too large. As the mixture is very light, care must be taken with the baking.

TORTOISE GATEAU.

The base and the body of the animal is made of Genoese, the head and flappers of marzipan.
The body is coated with coffee fondant and piped in chocolate.

ORANGE CAKES

This cake may be made in any shaped tins; the small six-sided tins now sold look very well and are novel.

1 lb. Sugar

1½ lbs. Eggs

$\frac{1}{4}$ lb. Butter
1 lb. Flour
Essence of Orange
Orange Colour.

Place the butter in a vessel on the oven stock to melt. Whisk up the sugar and eggs until thick, as for sponge cakes. Mix in the flour, essence, colour, and melted butter, taking care not to give it more work than necessary at this stage. Fill into prepared tins and bake in a fairly warm oven. When cold these cakes may be masked with orange flavoured fondant and the word "Orange" written in the proper colour, across it. A variety in this line may be made by using lemon juice and a light yellow colour, and calling the finished cake "Lemon."

RICH CAKE

This is a mixing that may be used for any class of rich fruit cake. Considerable numbers are sold in some shops, after being covered with a layer of almond paste :—

$2\frac{1}{2}$ lbs. Butter
$2\frac{1}{2}$ lbs. Sugar
$2\frac{1}{2}$ lbs. Eggs
$2\frac{3}{4}$ lbs. Flour
$\frac{1}{4}$ lb. Patent Flour
$1\frac{1}{2}$ lbs. Peel
$\frac{1}{2}$ lb. Almonds
2 lbs. Currants

1 lb. Sultanas
1 oz. Spice.

Cream up butter and sugar and beat in the eggs. Mix in the flour, fruit, etc., in the usual way, and if too dry, moisten with a little milk. Fill into round hoops or tins of the required size, and bake in a moderate oven.

SECTION XIII.

COUNTER GOODS RECIPES

QUEEN CAKES

THESE are ever popular cakes for ordinary trade, and every confectioner's shop should make a good show every day of goods of this class. In all small cakes, which are made in tins or moulds, it is of the first importance to see that the tins are cleaned and prepared in a proper manner. So many otherwise good-looking "smalls" are spoilt in appearance—by crummy corners, or by the use of an excess of fat in the preparation of the tins. Every tin should be carefully wiped out, and then thoroughly, but lightly, greased.

1. QUEEN CAKE

10 ozs. Butter
10 ozs. Sugar
6 Eggs
15 ozs. Flour
Currants
Volatile.

Cream up the butter and sugar thoroughly. Add the eggs, two at a time, beating them well in. Stir in the flour (into which a pinch

of volatile has been sifted).   Contrary to the usual custom, this mixing will do with a good "knock up" after the flour is in, and, as it
contains some volatile, it will then throw up a good "cauliflower"
top.   Fill the tins with a palette knife, in such a way as to make
the edges high and the middles quite low.   Put on a baking-sheet
and bake in a hot oven.   Some add the currants to the mixing,
others just sprinkle a few into the bay left in the middle of each cake
after filling.   Either method will do, but the former is preferred, as
in this case the currants run no risk of becoming charred in the hot
oven.

2. QUEEN CAKE

9 ozs. Butter
9 ozs. Sugar
7 Eggs
14 ozs. Flour
$\frac{1}{2}$ oz. Powder
Currants.

Proceed as before, not forgetting to give the mixing a good
knock up after the flour is added.   The excess of powder allows
for this.

3. QUEEN CAKE

1 lb. Butter
1 lb. Sugar
10 Eggs
1 lb. 6 ozs. Flour

$\frac{1}{2}$ oz. Powder

I lb. Currants

$\frac{1}{4}$ lb. Finely Chopped Peel.

Proceed as before.

ROCK CAKES, OR BUNS

2 lbs. Patent Flour

$\frac{1}{4}$ lb. Lard

$\frac{1}{2}$ lb. Sugar

$\frac{1}{2}$ lb. Currants

Pinch of Volatile

Milk

Rub the lard into the flour. Make a bay, into which put the other ingredients. Mix up with sufficient milk (buttermilk preferred) to make a slack dough. Break up into twenty even-sized pieces and place on a greased baking-sheet. The buns should be left quite rough, without any handing up, and may be washed with milk and dredged before being baked in a hot oven.

BRIGHTON ROCKS

6 lbs. Patent Flour

I$\frac{1}{2}$ lbs. Butter or Mixture

I$\frac{1}{2}$ lbs. Sugar

I lb. Sultanas

6 Eggs

A little Milk.

Proceed as before described. Make the dough very stiff, and see that the buns have a sufficiently rough appearance. This mixing ordinarily makes about ninety buns.

1. RICE BUNS

$1\frac{1}{2}$ lbs. Patent Flour
$\frac{1}{2}$ lb. Ground Rice
$\frac{1}{2}$ lb. Butter
$\frac{1}{2}$ lb. Sugar
5 Eggs
$\frac{1}{2}$ oz. Volatile (bare)
Milk.

Cream up the butter and sugar, and add the eggs gently, in the usual way. Sift the flour, ground rice, and volatile together, and mix the whole of the ingredients with a little milk into a soft dough. Scale off in pieces of about 2 ozs. each, and hand up on the board. Wash over the tops with a little milk and dip into fine sugar nibs. Place on greased baking-sheets and bake in a fairly hot oven.

2. RICE BUNS

2 lbs. Flour
$\frac{1}{4}$ lb. Ground Rice
1 oz. Powder
1 lb. Butter
1 lb. Sugar
10 Eggs.

Cream up the butter and sugar, and beat in the eggs. Sift the flour, ground rice, and powder together, and mix the whole with a little milk to a soft dough. Proceed as before directed.

RASPBERRY BUNS

2 lbs. Flour

$1\frac{1}{4}$ ozs. Powder

$\frac{1}{2}$ lb. Butter

10 ozs. Sugar

6 Eggs

About $\frac{1}{2}$ pint Milk

Raspberry Jam.

Cream up and mix precisely as for rice buns. When they are handed up on the board, flatten out each piece with the hand, and run over with a slightly damped wash-brush. Put a little raspberry jam in the middle of each piece of dough, and close up, by folding the sides over, and then pinching the damp edges together. Finish by washing the tops and dipping them in sugar nibs. Place on baking-sheets and bake in warm oven.

PRINCE OF WALES' BUN

3 lbs. Flour

1 oz. Powder

1 oz. Volatile

$\frac{1}{2}$ lb. Butter

$\frac{3}{4}$ lb. Sugar

9 Eggs
¾ lb. Currants
Milk.

Cream up in the usual way. Sift the flour and powders together, and then beat well up the whole of the ingredients with sufficient milk to make a fairly stiff batter. This should be stiff enough not to run when it is put on the pans, but no stiffer. Spoon out on greased baking-sheets. Lightly dredge and bake in a hot oven. If there is any fear of the bottom of these buns catching, double tin them when half baked.

COCOANUT BUNS

2¼ lbs. Flour
2 ozs. Powder
½ lb. Butter
10 ozs. Sugar
4 Eggs
6 ozs. Currants
2 ozs. Cocoanut
About 3 pints Milk.

Cream up in the usual way. Make up and pan in the same way as directed for Prince of Wales' buns. Wash over with egg and milk, sprinkle with cocoanut, and dredge with castor sugar. Bake in a hot oven, and be careful the bottoms do not scorch.

CORONATIONS

These cakes are made in small, flat, oblong tins, which are prepared by greasing lightly in the usual way.

$\frac{1}{2}$ lb. Butter

$\frac{1}{2}$ lb. Sugar

$\frac{3}{4}$ lb. Flour

$\frac{1}{4}$ lb. Currants

5 Eggs

Volatile

Citron.

Cream up in the usual way and fill into the tins, in the bottoms of which have been placed a strip of citron and a few currants. Bake in a moderate oven. When done, the cakes should be shown with the bottoms upward, exposing the citron and currants.

TURKEY BUNS

10 ozs. Butter

12 ozs. Sugar

6 Eggs

2 lbs. Flour

$1\frac{1}{2}$ ozs. Powder

$\frac{1}{4}$ pint Milk

Chopped Almonds.

Sift the flour and powder together. Cream up the butter and sugar, and add the eggs in the usual way. Mix in the flour, etc., and make up with milk. Lay out the buns on greased pans, wash, and sprinkle the tops with chopped almonds. Dredge lightly with sugar and bake in a fairly hot oven.

CHERRY CAKES

3 lbs. Flour
2 ozs. Powder
$\frac{3}{4}$ lb. Butter
14 ozs. Sugar
10 Eggs
$\frac{3}{4}$ lb. Cherries
$\frac{1}{2}$ pint Milk.

Chop up the cherries fairly fine. Sift the flour and the powder together. Cream up the butter and sugar, and add the eggs as usual. Make up with milk. Lay the buns out on greased pans, wash lightly, dredge with sugar, and place a half cherry on the top of each bun.

CHERRY CAKES

2 lbs. Flour
$\frac{1}{2}$ oz. Cream of Tartar
$\frac{1}{2}$ oz. Carbonate of Soda
8 ozs. Lard
2 ozs. Butter
10 ozs. Sugar
8 ozs. Cherries
2 Eggs

½ pint Milk
Pink Colouring.

Sift the flour and powder together. Rub in the butter and lard. Make a bay, into which put the sugar, eggs, milk, and colouring. This mixing should be coloured a bright pink. Make up into a soft dough. Weigh out in 1½ ozs. for four. Hand up on board. Wash lightly with milk and dip the tops into castor sugar. Lay out on greased baking-sheets, and put a quarter or half cherry on the top of each bun. Sell at a halfpenny each.

PARKIN

2 lbs. Flour
2 lbs. Pinhead Oatmeal
1 lb. Sugar
1 lb. Butter or Mixture
Ground Ginger
Spice (Mixed)
¾ oz. Soda Bicarbonate
Treacle
Almonds for tops.

Make the whole o the ingredients into a stiff paste with sufficient treacle for the purpose. The quantities of ginger and spice are purposely omitted, as they must be governed by individual tastes. Weigh off into 2-oz. pieces. Mould up into cone shapes, and wash over tops and sides with egg. Set on baking-sheets, placing each one 3 inches from the next. Put three half almonds on top of each parkin and bake in a cool oven. These goods flow down during baking, and, when done, are fairly thin. Sell at one penny each.

OATCAKE (THIN)

1 quart Pinhead Oatmeal
1 White of Egg
A little Salt
Water.

Mix the whole together into a firm paste. Break off in pieces about 6 ounces. Roll out thin, and cut into triangular pieces. Bake on clean baking-sheets. This is sold by the pound.

EASTERS

5 lbs. Flour
2½ lbs. Butter and Mixture
2½ lbs. Sugar
8 Eggs
Currants.

Rub the flour and butter fine. Make a bay, into which put the sugar and eggs. Mix up, with the addition of a little milk, into a firm dough, adding the currants whilst mixing. Roll out the paste fairly thin and cut out with a 4½-inch crimped cutter. Lay out on clean baking-sheets and bake in warm oven. This quantity should make seven dozen Easters at one penny each.

PLAIN BORDEAUX

$1\frac{1}{2}$ lbs. Butter
$1\frac{1}{2}$ lbs. Sugar
1 pint Eggs
2 lbs. Flour
A pinch of Powder
Some Orange Flavouring.

Cream up the butter and sugar in the usual way. Beat in the eggs. Mix in the flour, powder, flavouring, and a little milk (if necessary) to make the mixing fairly soft. Spread on a greased and papered baking-sheet, in the same manner as for Genoese, and bake in a moderate oven. When cold, cut into strips of a convenient size, and fondant the tops with different coloured fondants. Cut into fingers to sell at a penny each.

CHERRY BORDEAUX

1 lb. 2 ozs. Butter
1 lb. 2 ozs. Sugar
10 Eggs.
$2\frac{1}{4}$ lbs. Flour
$\frac{1}{4}$ oz. Powder
$\frac{1}{2}$ pint Milk
$\frac{3}{4}$ lb. Citron (cut into small cubes)
2 lbs. Cherries.

Proceed as for Plain Bordeaux. When cutting up this sheet of cake, use a very good knife, so that the cherries and citron may be cut quite clean. For this mixing use only white fondant.

PENNY SCHOOL CAKES

These are baked in similar tins to the penny Lunch.

> 3 lbs. Patent Flour
> ½ lb. Lard
> ¾ lb. Sugar
> 2 lbs. Currants
> Spice
> Little Volatile and sufficient Milk.

Rub the lard into the flour, and make a bay, and put in the sugar. Sprinkle the currants round the outside of bay. Dissolve the volatile and spice in a little drop of the milk and pour on the sugar. Mix all up to a medium consistency by adding whatever quantity of milk is required, and fill into small round tins.

PENNY LUNCH CAKES

These little cakes are usually baked in small round tins, and in appearance are miniature representations of larger lunch cakes.

> ½ lb. Butter
> ¾ lb. Sugar
> 6 Eggs
> 2½ lbs. Patent Flour
> About 1 pint of Milk
> Fruit as required.

Cream up the butter and sugar, and beat in the eggs. Mix in the flour and milk and whatever quantity of fruit may be desired. Fill into small round tins, dredge with sugar, and bake in a good sound oven.

SECTION XIV.

GINGERBREADS

GINGERBREAD is probably one of the oldest forms of confectionery existent. In nearly every country it is at some time of the year in considerable request, and is made and sold in large quantities. To such an old confection it is little wonder that traditions as to mode of manufacture have become attached, and consequently everybody seems to have their own ideas as to how their gingerbread should be made. Some retain the use of powerful chemicals, and allow what they call their prepared treacle to lie about in a trough for weeks, adding stiffening as required; whilst others go to the other extreme and mix their ingredients up quickly and bake off. Of these two methods the writers prefer the latter, but would in some cases advise a middle course. Before giving recipes it is well to point out that the somewhat widespread idea that anything, however rank, will do in gingerbread, is not to be encouraged, and that all the ingredients must be pure and wholesome.

QUEEN'S GINGERBREAD

This is a high-class gingerbread, which may be tastefully packed in tin foil, with a band round, and sold in good shops at a fair price.

3 lbs. Flour
$1\frac{3}{4}$ lbs. Sugar

½ lb. Butter
½ lb. Almonds (split)
½ lb. Peel (chopped)
¼ oz. Nutmeg
¼ oz. Mace
½ oz. Cinnamon
1 lb. Honey
1 lb. Syrup
1 oz. Ginger (Ground).

Rub the butter into the flour, and make a bay. Work the syrup and honey in the bay until quite slack and then put in the fruit, spices, etc. Mix all well together into a firm paste, and fill into a flat tin, such as a baking-sheet turned up all round. Level the top of the gingerbread with a rolling pin, and then with a wooden block (sold for the purpose) press on the paste, making some decorative design, which, when the cake is baked, will still be visible. Wash over with egg or sugar and water, and bake in a moderate oven. When cold, cut into squares and pack as before suggested.

BLOCK GINGERBREAD

8 lbs. Flour
2 lbs. Butter
1¼ lbs. Sugar
5 lbs. Syrup
2 lbs. Peel
2 ozs. Spice
2 ozs. Ginger

3 ozs. Soda Bicarbonate

1 pint Milk (about).

Rub the butter into the flour, make a bay, and mix in all the other ingredients. Work up into a stiffish dough and roll out about $1\frac{1}{2}$ inches thick on a baking-sheet as directed for Queen's Gingerbread.

GINGERBREAD FOR PENNY AND HALFPENNY SQUARES

$3\frac{1}{2}$ lbs. Flour

$1\frac{1}{4}$ lbs. Brown Sugar

$\frac{3}{4}$ lbs. Butter or Mixture

2 ozs. Ginger

$\frac{1}{2}$ oz. Powder (bare)

2 lbs. Treacle

$\frac{1}{2}$ oz. Allspice.

Mix the whole of the ingredients into a firm clear dough. Roll out about $\frac{1}{2}$ inch thick on a baking-sheet. Glaze by washing with egg, and bake in a moderate oven. Cut out into suitably-sized squares.

LARGE GINGER NUTS

$1\frac{3}{4}$ lbs. Flour

$\frac{1}{2}$ lb. Butter

$\frac{3}{4}$ lb. Sugar

1 oz. Ginger

Treacle
Pinch of Carbonate of Soda.

Mix the other ingredients into a medium soft dough. Let the dough stand in bulk for a short time, then break off lumps of about $\frac{1}{2}$ lb. each and roll out under hand into long rolls of about 1 inch diameter. Cut off into pieces about 1 inch long and stand on end on a greased baking-sheet. Take care not to place too close together, as the biscuits flow out. Bake in a moderate oven.

2. GINGER NUTS

6 lbs. Flour
$1\frac{1}{2}$ lbs. Butter
2 lbs. Sugar
1 quart Treacle
2 ozs. Ginger
$\frac{1}{2}$ oz. Powder.

Proceed as before.

SNAP GINGERBREADS

These goods are made and sold either curled or flat. The method is precisely the same up to the time of taking from the oven. When for curling, they are taken from the pan immediately on taking from the oven and turned over a rolling-pin, or, better still, a peel-handle, which has been slightly oiled. The biscuit on cooling quickly sets, and then becomes very brittle. All this class of goods must be kept in a dry, cool place.

7 lbs. Flour
2 lbs. Butter
8 lbs. Sugar
5½ pints Treacle
2 ozs. Ground Ginger
2 ozs. Allspice.

Mix all together and let lie for twenty-four hours. Break off in small pieces about the size of a small walnut, and bake on greased pans in a cool oven. This mixing flows very much, so care must be taken to keep each piece of dough at sufficient distance from the others. If preferred, the dough may be rolled and cut out with a round cutter, but the first method is quicker.

2. GINGER SNAPS

1 lb. Flour
½ lb. Butter
1 lb. Sugar
1 lb. Syrup
Ginger.

Proceed as before.

PENNY GINGERS

This is quite a different article to the previous recipes, as no treacle is used.

1½ lbs. Flour
½ lb. Butter
10 ozs. Sugar

2 Eggs
A little Milk
Some Ground Ginger.

Rub the butter into the flour, make a bay, into which put the other ingredients and sufficient milk to make into a medium dough. The quantity of ginger is not given, as tastes differ so much, that what is right in one shop is wrong in another, and as on the ginger added depends the name of the cake, the quantity is left to the discretion of the workman. Roll out the dough to about $\frac{3}{8}$ inches in thickness and cut out with a crimped cutter. Bake in a moderate oven on greased baking-sheets.

FRENCH GINGERBREAD

2 lbs. Flour
6 ozs. Butter
$\frac{1}{2}$ lb. Sugar
2 Eggs
1 oz. Powder
1 lb. Treacle
2 ozs. Sultanas
2 ozs. Peel (chopped)
Ground Ginger.

Rub the butter into the flour, make a bay, and put in the eggs and sugar. Work up the eggs and sugar together, and then put the other ingredients into the bay. Mix up into a clear dough and weigh off at about 2 ozs. each. Hand up. Roll out so that the two ends are small, as for Penny Shortbreads. Flatten out centre by pressing with palm of hand. Wash over with milk and bake on greased pans.

GINGER CAKES

2¾ lbs. Flour
½ oz. Powder
10 ozs. Butter
¾ lb. Sugar
2 lbs. Syrup
2 ozs. Ground Ginger
A pint of Milk.

Sift the powder into the flour, rub the butter into the flour, make a bay, and put in the other ingredients; or, as the mixing is soft, put the syrup, sugar, milk, and ginger into a mixing bowl, and add the flour, into which the butter has been rubbed. Mix thoroughly and fill into well-greased, small oblong tins. These cakes do best when baked in tins holding about ½ lb. to ¾ lb. of the mixture. Bake in a moderate oven.

SECTION XV.

VARIOUS PASTES

IN making most kinds of paste the butter or other fat is the chief ingredient, and this must be of good quality, sweet, and firm. The slightest taint or poverty in the butter shows itself very quickly in the finished articles. A good brand of Hungarian flour will be found most useful for the majority of pastes, as the peculiar brightness and tightening qualities of this flour are inimitable.

PUFF PASTE

This is one of the most important pastes which we have in constant use, and yet it is one of those articles which appear— through carelessness in manufacture—to be neglected. Every confectioner is supposed to make puff paste; but many otherwise good workmen fail through insufficient attention to exact details and to choice of ingredients to turn out a good show in this line. Where butter is mentioned in the following mixtures, other fat may be used.

Whilst always advocating the use of pure butters, we have no prejudice against any reliable mixture, which must leave no rank flavour or smell after cooking. In very hot weather some pastry mixtures are a great boon, as they keep much firmer and are less liable to be affected by the heat than the pure article.

RECIPE, No. 1

2 lbs. Butter
2 lbs. Flour
Water
Lemon Juice.

Weigh and sift the flour on the slab; make a bay, and put in sufficient cold water and a few drops of lemon juice. Work up into a dough, and work down well under hand to make thoroughly smooth, and of about the consistency of the butter. Allow the paste to lie on the slab whilst the butter is prepared. The butter should then be well worked by hand until the lump is of even consistency, and dust it with flour. Roll out the paste and put the butter in the middle. Press the mass of butter out evenly, turning the ends and sides of the paste over until the butter is covered, and press out with the hand. It is wise now, if time allows, to let the paste lie for about fifteen minutes, after which it must be rolled out in the following way. Roll right out to a long even strip and fold over into three, by first turning down the top edge to the three-quarter mark and then covering with the remaining flap from the bottom. The paste should then be turned half way round and the operation repeated, in each case taking care that the butter does not squeeze out. This is called a double turn. The paste then requires another short rest, then the operation is repeated. For ordinary puff paste three double turns are necessary, but experience soon shows if more are needed. The paste is then ready for use, and may be cut out as required. Bake in a quick oven.

The following recipes are simply varieties of the foregoing, and the method of manufacture is exactly the same, except when otherwise specified.

PUFF PASTE, No. 2

2 lbs. Flour
2 lbs. Butter
Water
A pinch of Cream of Tartar.

Before making the dough of flour and water, take $\frac{1}{2}$ lb. butter and rub into the flour. The remaining butter is rolled in as before described.

PUFF PASTE, No. 3

2 lbs. Flour
$1\frac{1}{2}$ lbs. Butter
Water
A pinch of Cream of Tartar.

This is sometimes called "three-quarter paste," and may be used for puffs, Banburys, etc. Rub in $\frac{1}{4}$ lb. butter and roll in the remainder as directed in No. 1.

OTHER METHODS

Viennese cooks often use the yolks of one or two eggs in their puff paste; and when this is done the yolks are mixed in at the same time as the water. For vol-au-vents and other fine pastry it is sometimes customary to use $1\frac{1}{4}$ lbs. butter to 1 lb. flour, but this requires great care in rolling and folding to prevent the butter squeezing out; it should also be given several more " turns."

In all varieties of puff paste give exact attention to details. The folding must be done evenly and regularly to ensure that the finished goods may be upright and the flakes in the pastry may be perfect. After cutting out tartlets, cheesecakes, etc., for baking on flat sheets, it is as well to turn each piece over before placing on tin, as the operation of cutting out makes the top edge smaller than the bottom edge, and the tartlet is in consequence much smaller at the top than the bottom.

1. SHORT PASTE

This paste may be used for custards, short paste tartlets, and many other purposes. It can be made in many qualities, and can be cheapened or otherwise at any time by altering the quantities of butter and eggs.

Our first recipe is for a sweet paste, and can only be used for sweet goods, such as mentioned above.

> 2 lbs. Flour
> 1 lb. Butter
> 2 ozs. Sugar
> 3 Eggs
> $\frac{1}{4}$ pint Water.

Rub the butter into the flour. Make a bay, into which is put the sugar, eggs, and water. Mix thoroughly and make smooth.

2. SHORT PASTE

This may be used for covering pies, or any other purpose for which sugar is undesirable.

> 1 lb. Flour
> 1 lb. Patent Flour

1 lb. Butter
A little Salt
Water.

Rub the butter into the flour and add salt. Mix up with sufficient water to the right consistency.

SHORT PASTE FOR FRENCH PIES

This paste is used for lining the inside of French Pie Moulds for game pies, etc. It is a fairly rich mixing, and although quite simple, is exceedingly popular for this purpose.

10 ozs. Butter
1 lb. Flour
1 Egg
A little Water
A little Salt.

Rub the butter and flour together until fine, and work up into a smooth dough by adding the egg and sufficient water.

GERMAN PASTE

This is a sweet paste which is used as a base for many fancy goods. It can be utilised in many ways, and a small supply ready mixed should be kept in a cool place for use at any time.

3 lbs. Flour
2 lbs. Butter
1 lb. Sugar
4 Eggs.

Rub the butter into the flour until fine, and work up into a stiff paste by adding eggs and sugar.   In this, as in all other pastes, care must be taken not to dust the paste with too much flour after it is once mixed.   If too much flour is used for this purpose, it is well to keep a brush near at hand, and to carefully brush before using or folding.

1. PORK PIE PASTE

4 lbs. Flour
1½ lbs. Lard
1 oz. Salt
1 pint Water.

Boil the water and lard, and when boiling pour on to the flour, which must be quickly mixed up into a paste with a spatula.   Work down under hand until smooth, and then set aside to cool.

Or this

PORK PIE PASTE

4 lbs. Flour
1¼ lbs. Lard
¼ lb. Butter
1 oz. Salt
1 pint Water.

Rub the butter into the flour and make into a bay.   Boil the lard with the water, and when boiling pour into the bay.   Mix up, with the spatula, into a paste, and set aside to cool.

SECTION XVI.

FILLINGS FOR CAKES

LEMON HONEY, OR LEMON CHEESE CURD

Juice of 8 Lemons
8 Eggs
1 lb. Sugar
½ lb. Butter
¾ pint Water.

PUT all the ingredients in a stew-pan over the fire, and keep well stirred till the mixture boils. Let it boil for two minutes.

FILLING FOR MACAROON TARTLETS

(ALSO CALLED CONGRESS CAKES OR TARTS, ALMOND TARTS, ETC.)

6 Whites
6 ozs. Sugar
4 ozs. Ground Almonds
1 oz. Cones.

Whisk the whites, but not too stiff, then add the other ingredients, and fill into the cases.

RICHMOND MAIDS OF HONOUR

¾ lb. Sugar
12 Yolks
¾ lb. Butter

2 G

2 ozs. Fine Cocoanut
1 pint Milk
Tablespoonful of Rennet
Nutmeg.

Mode:—Mix yolks and sugar well with whisk. Melt the butter and pour in. Warm the milk and rennet till thick, and lay out on a sieve to drain, then rub it through the sieve into the mixture; add the cocoanut and grated nutmeg, and fill into the cases.

GOOD ALMOND FILLING

-1 lb. Almonds
1 lb. Sugar
¼ lb. Butter
6 or 8 Yolks.

Mix the almonds and sugar with the yolks, and beat well together with a spattle. Meanwhile run the butter down in a cup in the mouth of the oven, and pour slowly into the mixture, stirring it well in. More or less yolks may be necessary, according to their size and the consistency at which the filling is required. This makes a nice eating centre in Othellos and Indianas, for sandwiching Genoese, and also for covering the tops of the latter before sprinkling with brown chopped almonds.

HUNGARIAN CREAM

1 lb. Lump Sugar
¾ lb. Butter
10 Yolks
2 ozs. Cocoa
Vanilla Bean.

Place the sugar with some water and the vanilla pod in a stew-pan and allow to boil to the "blow" degree. While it is boiling, cream the butter—which must be of the very best—in one bowl and whisk up the yolks in another. Pour the boiling syrup slowly on the yolks, beating all the while, and add the melted chocolate. It should then be beaten until cool, and poured on the creamed butter, stirring the while with a wooden spoon.

BRABANTER CREAM

This is made in the same manner as the Hungarian, but with the addition of a ¼ lb. of whole almonds, which are first browned in the oven, then pounded in a mortar with a little milk (to prevent them from "oiling") until it forms a smooth paste. This is then added to the creamed butter and thoroughly mixed; it gives the cream an additional flavour, and is a great favourite with many people.

BUTTER CREAM FILLING

The ordinary butter cream is made from equal quantities of best butter and icing sugar. The butter should first be well creamed, and the sugar gradually added and beaten in. This forms a nice light cream, which is quickly made, and is very useful for fillings, or for covering.

A better and richer cream is made in the same way, but with the addition of a few yolks of eggs, which materially add to the eating qualities of the filling.

The mixing should be divided into as many portions as there are flavours required; Vanilla will be found the favourite, though coffee butter cream is very much liked, and, when made from strong fresh-made coffee, is excellent.

Chocolate cream is made by the addition of a little melted block chocolate and essence of Vanilla.

TOUTI FRUITI CREAM

This makes a nice eating centre for fruit gateaux, and is out of the ordinary run.   A cream should be made from—

> 1 lb. Sugar
> 1 lb. Butter
> 5 or 6 Yolks
> Mixed Preserved Fruits.

The fruits must be chopped to a suitable size.   A smoother cream is to be obtained by boiling the sugar, adding to the yolks, and, when cool, mixing in with the butter.

MARRONS FILLING

When making marrons glacés there is generally a considerable quantity of pieces which are too broken to be of any use for sale purposes.   When these are saved they make a splendid eating centre for the Petits Fours Glacés of the Othello mixings.

They can be mixed in with the butter cream in the same way as the fruit, or they can be used as they are by pressing into a paste with the hands.   The syrup left after making marrons glacés should also be utilised, as it has an excellent flavour.

PUNCH FILLING

Take rubbed down Genoese cuttings and mix well with enough simple syrup and rum to form a paste. Many gateaux are made on the Continent with a Genoese top and bottom, and this filling an inch thick through the centre. The rum flavour is very much liked when used in this way.

COCOANUT FILLING

Cocoanut being so well liked by a portion of the public, the following will, no doubt, be found to sell well in certain districts. Take—

8 Whites
1 lb. Sugar
½ lb. Desiccated Cocoanut.

Whisk the whites, add the sugar and cocoanut, and put in a bowl on the fire, keeping the mixture from burning by stirring from the bottom. Have the gateau or strips ready sliced, and when the mixture is hot, pour on and spread level, then place on the tops.

NEAPOLITAN CREAM

This is the usual butter cream, laid through strips of Genoese or gateaux in three layers, each one being a distinct colour and flavour, the gateaux or fancies taking the name "Neapolitan." A nice eating cream is formed by adding a quantity of sponge cake crumbs to butter cream, with the advantage of being cheaper by using up what might probably be waste cake.

CASTANIAN FILLING

Procure some good chestnuts and boil them in water until soft, then remove the jackets and rub the nuts through a sieve. Work sufficient fine castor with some Vanilla sugar into them to make a paste. Care should be taken not to work in too much, or the paste will be soft. This makes a splendid eating filling for Petits Fours, etc.

CUSTARD JELLY

Boiled custard makes a good filling for many small pastries, choux, various sandwiches, Indianas, etc. It is needless to mention that it needs a quick sale, as it will not keep any length of time. The following makes a nice mixture for centres :—

> 10 Yolks
> 6 ozs. Sugar
> 1 oz. Corn-flour
> $1\frac{1}{2}$ pints Milk.

Whisk the yolks and then the other ingredients together, place in a stew-pan and stir till it is just on the boil. Another, and perhaps a better, method is to boil the milk, pour it on the yolks and sugar, stirring all the time, and then to return the whole to the stew-pan, and place on the fire till nearly boiling. Care must be taken that it does not burn. It requires to be made thicker for some purposes than for others. The corn-flour should be mixed with a little cold milk before adding to the mixture. Flavour with Vanilla.

WHIPPED CREAM

Whipped cream is always the leading favourite for Cream Buns, Eclaires, etc., although it is not applied to so many varieties of goods in this country as on the Continent, where many gateaux are filled, completely masked, and even piped with it; small fancies, etc., being served in a somewhat similar fashion. The whipping of the cream is a simple operation, though considerable care is sometimes required, especially during hot weather, when it will be found necessary to place the bowl containing the cream on ice whilst whisking.

STRAWBERRY CREAM

Whipped cream, with whole wild strawberries mixed with it, makes a very choice centre for a Crême gateau, and the top should be decorated with the same fruit.

VARIOUS MERINGUE FILLINGS

Perhaps the most useful and cheapest of all fillings is meringue, for it serves so many purposes and goes such a long way. It needs to be well made, and *thick*, not *light* only, or it will very soon run back; this is only to be achieved by beating the sugar well in. It is used for the tops and centres of gateaux, and a large variety of small pastries and Genoese, some of which are shown amongst the illustrations. To form a centre for hazelnut Genoese, sufficient ground nuts should be mixed in to give it a nutty flavour. When melted, fine chocolate is added, and the meringue stiffens a little, and thus forms a stronger substance for the purpose of spreading on strips of chocolate Genoese, which can then be cut in suitable sizes and dipped in chocolate fondant or icing.

FILLING FOR FANCY PASTRIES

Boil a pound of apples till soft, pour off the water, add the same quantity of sugar, a drop of lemon flavour, and 2 ozs. of gelatine, and again boil for ten minutes.

ALMOND CHEESE CURD

$\frac{1}{2}$ lb. Butter
$\frac{1}{2}$ lb. Sugar
$\frac{1}{2}$ lb. Eggs
$\frac{1}{2}$ lb. Cake-crumbs
$\frac{1}{4}$ lb. Ground Almonds.

Cream the butter and sugar, adding the eggs two at a time, and stir in the crumbs and ground almonds.

CHEESE CURD

The following is a cheaper mixing for a cheese curd filling than that given in the foregoing recipe :—

$\frac{1}{4}$ lb. Butter
$\frac{1}{2}$ lb. Sugar
4 Eggs
$\frac{1}{2}$ lb. Cake-crumbs
Nutmeg.

INDEX

W